T0170618

OLD ALABAMA TOWN

MARY ANN NEELEY

OLD ALABAMA TOWN

AN ILLUSTRATED GUIDE

Published in cooperation with Landmarks Foundation of Montgomery

THE UNIVERSITY OF ALABAMA PRESS
Tuscaloosa and London

Copyright © 2002
The University of Alabama Press
Tuscaloosa, Alabama 35487-0380
All rights reserved
Manufactured in the United States of America

Designed by Robin McDonald

Typeset in Bauer Bodoni

∞

The paper on which this book is printed meets the minimum requirements of American National Standard for Information Science–Permanence of Paper for Printed Library Materials, ANSI Z39.48-1984.

Unless otherwise noted, photographs of Old Alabama Town are by Robin McDonald and used courtesy of the photographer.

Library of Congress Cataloging-in-Publication Data

Neeley, Mary Ann.
  Old Alabama Town : an illustrated guide / Mary Ann Neeley.
      p. cm.
"Published in cooperation with Landmarks Foundation of Montgomery."
Includes bibliographical references.
  ISBN 0-8173-1179-3 (alk. paper)
 1. Old Alabama Town (Montgomery, Ala.) 2. Historic sites—Alabama—Montgomery. 3. Montgomery (Ala.)—History—19th century. 4. Montgomery (Ala.)—Social life and customs—19th century. 5. Montgomery (Ala.)—Buildings, structures, etc. I. Landmarks Foundation of Montgomery (Montgomery, Ala.) II. Title.
  F334.M76.O43 N44 2002
  976.1'4705—dc21

                                        2002003839

British Library Cataloguing-in-Publication Data available

CONTENTS

ACKNOWLEDGMENTS

S o many have contributed to the inception and development of Old Alabama Town that it is impossible to name all, but without their efforts there would be no tales to spin and, of course, no book. The "Founding Fathers" include the late Milo B. Howard, state archivist, historian, preservationist, and James L. Loeb, Montgomery businessman and visionary. Recognizing the need for the preservation of our architectural heritage, they encouraged others of like interests; Landmarks Foundation and Old Alabama Town are the fruits of their inspiration and labors.

Support from mayors Earl James, Jim Robinson, Emory Folmar, and Bobby Bright, from members of the city council, county commission, and from municipal employees has been instrumental in the success of this endeavor. The dedication and determination of the members of Landmarks Foundation Board of Directors, the staff, crew, and volunteers of the Foundation, and the citizens of Montgomery have provided the energy that continues to propel this project on its unswerving course.

Now, on a personal note, I want to thank all of the above for their direction, support, and encouragement during this incredible adventure I have enjoyed for the past twenty-five years. In addition, I deeply and gratefully appreciate the assistance I have received in the preparation of this book. The Landmarks Foundation personnel and my family and friends have exhibited untold patience, tolerance, and understanding.

Several individuals including Edith Crook, Dr. Thomas Oliver, James Loeb, and Alta Cassady have read, listened, and offered sound advice and objective criticism. Robert Gamble, architectural historian, has generously answered numerous questions, and I should have asked him many more. Dr. Thomas Oliver prepared maps, as did Robert Bonn.

In the final analysis, however, the responsibility remains that of the author. Voltaire said, in effect, that someone who tries to write an accurate history will be attacked for everything he says and for everything he does not say. So be it.

MONTGOMERY IN THE NINETEENTH CENTURY

A HISTORICAL OVERVIEW

I t was 1793 and the fate of the Creek Indians and their central Alabama homeland hung in the balance. In February, Alexander McGillivray, the dynamic half Scot and half Indian leader of the Creek Nation, died with no heir apparent. During the same period, a young New Englander, Eli Whitney, was recovering from smallpox on a coastal Georgia plantation and, perhaps in return for the hospitality tendered, began working on an engine for separating cotton lint from its tenaciously clinging seed. No one realized at the time that these two events were shaping the future of a land and its people—Native American, Euro-American, and African American.

Alexander McGillivray had taken control of a shaken Creek Confederacy whose leaders had given its allegiance to Great Britain during the Revolutionary War; at its conclusion he realized that the support and trade goods so desperately needed would no longer be forthcoming from its old ally. Working with Spanish and English merchants, McGillivray adroitly guided the Creeks from the departure of the British in 1783 until his death, taking on the land-hungry Americans with little fear and great gusto. Without him, though, the Native Americans lacked strong leadership in a territory deemed almost perfect for the growing of cotton, a fiber in worldwide demand since the Industrial Revolution's mechanization of textile manufacturing.

The lint and seed of long-staple cotton that grew along the coast separated easily, but the same elements of the short-staple cotton clung to each other. The inland areas of the South offered perfect conditions for the short staple's growth; however, cultivating it was not economically feasible unless there were means of quickly and efficiently removing the seed. Throughout the region, people were working frantically to perfect a machine to carry out the task.

Campbell-Holtzclaw Cottage

Whitney, a recent graduate of Yale, was a guest at Mulberry Grove Plantation near Savannah and became interested in the need. It is unclear how much of the work had been done by others, but Whitney had the foresight to apply for a patent for his gin, an engine that separated the two components and made the cultivation of short-staple cotton practical and profitable. Perfect land for the crop was plentiful in the interior, but the Creeks occupied it as they had for centuries.

For the next twenty years the tension on the old southwest frontier grew and festered until 1814 when Andrew Jackson defeated the Creeks at the Battle of Horseshoe Bend, forcing them to cede millions of acres of central Alabama lands to the United States. They reserved for themselves lands west of the Chattahoochee and east of the Coosa Rivers. The recently acquired region soon swarmed with intrepid and adventuresome American pioneers who traveled down the Federal Road, an old Indian path widened initially as a post road for commu-

nication between Washington and New Orleans. "Alabama Fever" raged with the intensity of the plague as thousands set out for the newly opened territory with cotton on their minds. Their enthusiasm is easy to understand as cotton was selling in New Orleans at 29.8 cents a pound.

In 1819 the Alabama Territorial Legislature incorporated two small villages, founded when the cession went on sale in 1817, as Montgomery. Born a

Approach to Montgomery, Alabama—1870 *by A. R. Waud*

child of the Industrial Revolution and the War of 1812, the town grew up on
the banks of the Alabama River, the grand avenue that linked central Alabama to the Gulf of Mexico and to the world. Developing as a trade and transportation center for the surrounding farms and plantations, it soon supported

merchants, craftsmen, and professionals all of whom depended, in one way or another, on cotton. The economy rested upon it, sometimes with great ease and at other times precariously.

River traffic became increasingly busy with the arrival of steamboats in 1821. Cotton moved downstream faster, and more merchandise arrived for merchants and other buyers. In the early 1830s entrepreneurs began a railroad to Georgia, and even though it took nineteen years to complete, the line quickly began to bring cotton in from outlying areas to city warehouses and for shipping on steamboats. With its successful completion and the subsequent building of other railroads, train travel eventually would supersede that on the river.

Throughout the era, cotton drove the economy, and the acquisition of more property upon which to grow it brought about the final demise of the Creek Nation in central Alabama. The natives had reserved for themselves a home in the 1814 settlement, but an 1832 treaty assured their removal to the western territories of the United States where the federal government provided lands for them. The Alabama state line was now at the Chattahoochee River. Another land rush began in central Alabama, and by 1837 the development of farms and plantations in the new counties to the east of Montgomery was well under way. This in combination with increasing population and wealth in the Black Belt placed the town in a most fortunate position near the demographic and geographic center of the state.

Tuscaloosa, state capital since 1825, was now in the western part of the state, too inaccessible for some. An 1845 referendum announced the voters' consent to consider moving the state offices to a more central location. After much lobbying and hotly contested voting in the legislature, Montgomery finally captured the honor, with announcement of the victory reaching the jubilant new seat of government on 30 January 1846. As part of its enticement, the city donated Goat Hill, a hill at the eastern end of Market Street reserved by visionary founding father Andrew Dexter, as a site for the capitol; funds for the building would come from a $75,000 bond issue floated by Montgomery and its citizens.

Philadelphia architect Stephen Decatur Button designed the new "Temple of Democracy," which graced the spot where formerly goats had grazed. Sadly, it burned to the ground in 1849, but within two years the state had constructed another, built on the foundations of the old.

Montgomery thrived in its new role, adding politics to trade and transportation, while cotton still continued its inexorable power over the thoughts and actions of Alabamians. With good cotton prices as underpinning, during the 1850s the town put on a new air of sophistication, improving city services and building fashionable residences, commercial houses, and churches. Gas lighting and the completion of the railroad to Georgia enhanced the quality of life for much of the population.

Prosperity continued with the price of cotton remaining respectable even through the Panic of 1857, but there was trouble on the horizon. Following the Mexican War and the acquisition of new territories, differences between an industrialized North and an agrarian South and between slave states and free states were mounting; the issue of slavery had to be resolved.

As abolitionists and advocates of halting the extension of slavery gained ascendancy outside the South, ardent states rights advocates such as Montgomerian William Lowndes Yancey proclaimed the right of secession. Unable to gain acceptance of his proposals for the protection of slavery in the new territories and states, Yancey led the southern delegations out of the Democratic Convention of 1860, splintering the party and paving the way for the election of Abraham Lincoln.

Secession quickly followed, and Alabama withdrew from the Union on 11 January 1861. In early February, delegates from southern states met in the capitol and organized the Confederate States of America with Montgomery chosen as the provisional capital and Jefferson Davis as president.

It was a heady experience for the small city of 8,800 citizens. Some welcomed the influx of people with open arms and homes, but for others it was an ordeal followed by a sense of relief when the government moved to Richmond, Virginia, in May. War came with the firing on Fort Sumter on 12 April, and the leaders of the Confederacy felt that they should be close to the battlefields for what they expected to be a short conflict.

Montgomery settled into an important role as a supplier of men and materials. Railroads and their shops worked night and day, making repairs to equipment and moving goods to the battlefields and other beleaguered southern regions. Production of military ware included guns and ironclads, the latter built in a slough next to the city wharf. As a relatively safe place, the town was ideal for hospitals, and during the four war years, there were six, located in a private homes, commercial buildings, and tent camps. Men from Montgomery served in major and minor battles, some losing limbs and others their lives. Details from the front lines arrived at the telegraph office in the Winter Building on Court Square where anxious families and friends waited around the Artesian Basin to hear the casualty lists as operators read the doleful news from the second-floor veranda.

All the efforts, however, were futile for after the Battle of Selma in early April 1865 the small Confederate force in Montgomery moved out, knowing they could not deter the advance of General James H. Wilson's Cavalry Corps. Before leaving, however, they agreed with the City Council to burn the 80,000 to 100,000 bales of cotton stored in Montgomery warehouses by planters and farmers who awaited the end of the blockade and the embargo to ship their valuable holdings to hungry mills. At 5 P.M. on 11 April the torching began, and soon afterward the mayor and councilmen rode out to surrender the city. (In 1860, cotton sold in New Orleans for 11.1 cents per pound. Based on inflation, today 100,000 bales would be worth more than a half-billion dollars.)

Wilson gave strict orders for the protection of citizens and their property, but he had all military-related sites and materials destroyed. Montgomerians were fortunate in that the built environment was virtually intact as people began to reestablish their lives with all having to make accommodations for the political, social, and economic changes that were at hand.

Former slaves moved into town, swelling the population to the saturation point with some living on the outskirts in shacks made out of scrap materials from the burned railroad shops. In the fall and winter of 1865, smallpox broke out among the new arrivals, many of whom had never been vaccinated. The season was harsh and miserable for most. Local authorities, the Freedmen's Bureau, American Missionary Association, and charitable groups worked to alleviate suffering throughout town. With the help of these groups, the organization of institutions such as schools and churches was soon under way.

The decade following the war changed the political landscape with Republican mayors and African Americans serving on the Montgomery City Council. Political reconstruction, however, ended in the mid-1870s with the reelection of the old guard on city and state levels.

Cotton was still king although somewhat sullied in the eyes of those who urged crop diversification. Throughout central Alabama, landowners needed labor to raise crops, and thousands of people needed places to live and work. Sharecropping, although decried by the National Grange for the Patrons of Husbandry and other farmers' movements, did offer a solution for everyone. A rural majority found a living as "croppers" and tenants, answering the siren call of cotton's constant bid for attention as the only means of making a little cash.

Within the city, technology presented one miracle after another as the 1880s brought about a second period of urbanization. Telephones and electric lights heralded a decade that also witnessed the advent of an electric trolley system, the first in the nation. Water, too, played a leading role with a new water works and the erection of the magnificent baroque fountain in Court Square.

While all segments of the population enjoyed these innovations, the urban African-American population was experiencing a surge of progress and even prosperity. Educational opportunities increased with State Normal School, the Montgomery Girls Industrial School, and other public and private institutions. Churches, too, proliferated with one of the most prominent, the Second Baptist Church, constructing an edifice within a block of the capitol building. Professionals, businessmen, and educators strengthened the whole community and contributed to a prevailing and growing confidence. Optimism reached a peak with the visit of Grover Cleveland in October 1887. The first Democratic president since the Civil War, he received a rousing welcome during his one-day visit. The exhilaration, however, did not last with the financial woes of the early 1890s creating a number of anxieties triggered locally by the collapse of the city's largest business, Moses Brothers Banking and Realty Co.

Even so, a new spirit, infused by the growth of the wholesale industry and flourishing railroad operations, soon manifested itself. Contributing to this were the forty passenger trains that came into the city daily, bringing customers and clients with money, ideas, and aspirations. To better serve these travelers, the Louisville and Nashville Railroad built the magnificent Union Station and train shed that opened in May 1898, just in time for the departure of men for the Spanish-American War.

The war with Spain did not last long nor did the full impact of it and *Plessy vs. Ferguson*, the 1896 Supreme Court edict of "separate but equal," register immediately on the country. The almost simultaneous emergence of American imperialism and Jim Crow (the disenfranchisement of a majority of blacks and many whites and legal barriers to separate the races) ushered in the twentieth century which would have to deal with both.

As the century closed on central Alabama, cotton remained on the throne, sometimes painfully so, but nobody was as yet overly concerned about the small obnoxious boll weevil that slowly, irrevocably, was moving this way from Mexico. They, too, were to be major factors in the lives of Alabamians who viewed the vast, promising horizon of the twentieth century with both hope and trepidation.

INTRODUCTION TO LANDMARKS FOUNDATION OF MONTGOMERY

An oft-repeated axiom states that by learning about the past we can better appreciate the present and can better prepare for the future. Since the Mount Vernon's Ladies Association was organized in 1853 to save the home of George Washington, Americans have placed a value on the architectural elements of our past as aids in understanding our national, regional, and local history. Sometimes, as in the case of Mount Vernon, structures serve as shrines. In other instances, they reflect the cultural standards, ideals, and, for the most part, the needs and tastes distinct to a particular group of people.

Alabamians have a reverence for the past. During the early years of the twentieth century many gave their support to women of the state who, working with their southern sisters, saved the First White House of the Confederacy—the home of Jefferson Davis and his family when Montgomery was the capital of the Confederate States.

During the 1930s, the federal government funded the Historic American Building Survey which provided out-of-work architects and historians with much needed employment and gave the nation invaluable drawings, photographs, and histories of buildings, many of which are now gone. Since 1966 when the federal government passed the Historic Preservation Act, state and local governments have followed with laws that recognize the value of preserving the tangible evidence of our history. These laws have enabled us to devote time, energy, and money to the appreciation, assessment, and preservation of our built environment.

In the 1960s, as interstates and urban renewal tore at the fabric of neighborhoods and city streets, the nationwide preservation movement began in earnest.

Alabama's legislature passed enabling laws, permitting municipalities to establish boards through which important sites and structures could be noted and protected. In 1967 the Montgomery City Commission enacted ordinances creating the Montgomery Historical Development Commission (HDC) and, its companion, the Architectural Review Board (ARB). The following year, at the suggestion of City Attorney Horace Perry, a nonprofit corporation, Landmarks Foundation of Montgomery, Inc., was organized with its mission being the preservation and the interpretation of local history, architecture, and lifestyle. Joining hands with the city, Landmarks Foundation set its course.

House museums proliferated around the country and were ideal for the interpretation of architecture, history, and life in the past. On North Hull Street the Ordeman-Shaw House, with its kitchen and slave quarters, was for sale. It was a prime candidate for restoration as a house museum and, at the same time, to serve as a model for other interested state and city groups to emulate. Mont-

A Gasolier illuminates the back parlor of the Ordeman House,
Old Alabama Town's crown jewel and first restoration.

gomery followed earlier patterns for house museums as it began its ventures into historic preservation.

The 1968 purchase of the Ordeman-Shaw House cemented the unique joining of a public and a private body. With a $100,000 Housing and Urban Development grant and private contributions, Landmarks Foundation and the city acquired and meticulously researched and restored the Italianate town house, its outbuildings, and its grounds. Opening to the public in 1971, the house became the nucleus around which Old Alabama Town has grown. Landmarks Foundation and the city have continued to work closely in the development of Old Alabama Town. It now consists of fifty buildings, the majority of which have been brought into the district for safekeeping.

Philosophically, while some take the position that it is sacrilege to move a structure from its original site, the Foundation believes that it is better to have a structure preserved for posterity than a stark chimney keeping a lonely vigil in an obscure, difficult to reach location. Certainly, the Foundation understands and appreciates in situ value, but they recognize that of these fifty structures, housed for preservation and the benefit of the public in Old Alabama Town, very few would still exist had they not been moved. Landmarks Foundation develops and administers the area meeting partial property acquisition and restoration costs with Community Development Block Grants and private funding. Its operational costs of the outdoor museum are met through rents, membership, tourism, the museum shop profits, and contributions.

Landmarks Foundation has encountered many challenges during the past thirty years and time and again has risen to the occasion, sometimes as activist and on others in an advisory capacity. Outside of Old Alabama Town, the Foundation has saved the Governor Shorter House, Knox Hall, House of the Mayors, Cody House, and the Confederate Post Office and has contributed money for the restoration of the National Historic Landmark Union Station Train Shed. It has also encouraged commercial restorations such as those along Commerce Street, and it became involved in the development of Cottage Hill and other residential renovations throughout the city.

The bellwether of Montgomery's preservation movement, Landmarks Foundation has served as a model for other organizations with similar missions. Today, it continues to provide leadership and assistance with dedication and enthusiasm for the task while using Old Alabama Town as a cultural resource and as a very important repository of southern architecture, history, and culture.

OLD ALABAMA TOWN

OLD ALABAMA TOWN

Old Alabama Town, the South's premier history village, welcomes you. If you are in Old Alabama Town, this book will help you identify the structures and will tell you about them, and if you are reading from home, it will allow you to vicariously experience this extraordinary place.

The Reception Center at 301 Columbus Street is the place to begin. A visit can be an hour, two hours, or all day; it really depends on you. We hope you will take your time savoring the grounds, the architecture, and the history of Old Alabama Town and enjoying the friendly people who work here. If you are exploring off-site, you will have almost the same opportunity to see the buildings and their architectural details and to read about the people who built and occupied the houses and workplaces. Old Alabama Town is about people, for is not history our story? Architecture, the most intimate of art forms, is solely for the benefit of and enjoyment by people. Here, architecture is the instrument through which we depict lifestyle and focus on how people lived and worked in an earlier Alabama. In the Working Block we see where and how people produced necessities, and in the Living Block we see and discuss places where people gathered together.

There are many possible ways to experience Old Alabama Town. If architecture is your primary interest, there is a veritable treasure here to tantalize and instruct. Maybe the main reason for your visit is history, and if that is the case, nearly two hundred years have stories to tell about Alabama's frontier, its settlement, its development, and the course of events from 1814 to the turn of the twentieth century.

Perhaps it is that elusive quality we all sometimes yearn for and seek—a connection to our individual and collective pasts—that lure us to such places as this. Old Alabama Town provides tangible memory with the sights, smells, sounds, and associations that stir our primal selves and help us remember who we are as individuals and as a people.

A palmetto fan and cotton bolls comment on the South's climate: the fan combats heat, while cotton thrives in it.

So often we hear, "my grandma had one just like this," and then we know that the washpot, or whatever the artifact in question, has helped accomplish the goal of vibrantly bringing the past into everyday lives. Smarter and more poetic folks than we have said it better, but "we are a part of all that we have met," personally and collectively and, as William Faulkner so aptly said, "the past is not dead, it's not even past." Old Alabama Town is here to remind us of this.

Our mission is to see that you have a good time while experiencing the past of central Alabama. No, we have not been able to cover every aspect of life nor do we have examples of every architectural style, but you will see a cross section of the way life was for Alabamians of all classes, races, and creeds. Have fun, offer your comments to us, and please tell others about Old Alabama Town, a nineteenth-century treasure.

Reception Center (301 Columbus Street)

This is your introduction to Old Alabama Town. Our knowledgeable receptionist will tell you about what is available, the touring schedules, admission, and how to get to the appropriate starting place. You may also wish to do some shopping in the museum store, and, of course, we always welcome that. The receptionist will give you clear, detailed instructions as to exactly where to start your tour and how to get there. Please enjoy the murals; "Alabama Time Line" and "Federal Road" will give you a background for your tour.

Living Block

If the Living Block is your first destination, upon leaving the Reception Center proceed up the sidewalk to North Hull Street. At the corner carefully cross Columbus Street and while walking along, observe the architecture of the cottages on both sides of the street. At the light, cross North Hull to Lucas Tavern, the white building with a flag flying in front.

At Lucas Tavern a costumed interpreter will greet you and take you on a tour of this fine old building. You will then receive a cassette with a tape narrated by Alabama's foremost storyteller, Kathryn Tucker Windham, which will lead you through the Living Block. You may meet other characters from the past, and if you do, turn off your tape and discuss their lives and times with them. On this tour are the arbor, dogtrot house, Grange Hall, carriage house, country doctor's office, shotgun house, corner grocery, church, schoolhouse, herb garden, pole barn, and log cabin.

Upon returning to Lucas Tavern, you will receive instructions for the next phase of the tour.

Working Block

If the Working Block is your first destination, upon leaving the Reception Center proceed up the sidewalk to North Hull Street, cross carefully, and walk up the asphalt sidewalk to the Rose House, the two-story building behind the stone wall and hedges. Here a guide will introduce you to the cotton gin, grist mill, blacksmith shop, print shop, drugstore museum, and the exhibits in the small outbuildings. Craftpersons and musicians will enhance the tour.

A costumed interpreter discusses the domestic chores that took place around the courtyard.

Ordeman House

The receptionist will tell you the time and place to meet for the Ordeman House tour. A guide will escort you through this exquisitely furnished 1850s Italianate town house. There are tours Monday through Saturday. If you should miss the Ordeman tour, you are welcome to come back within forty-eight hours.

Young House Restaurant

Monday to Friday enjoy having lunch in the historic Young House. The food is southern with an upscale touch. Fried chicken is, of course, always a main feature of any Deep South meal, but other entrees, sandwiches, and soups are also on the menu.

Again, welcome to the place where the past is always present and the future was yesterday.

OLD ALABAMA TOWN
MAP KEY

KIWANIS PARK BUILDINGS
1. Loeb Reception Center
2. Dorsey Cottage Shanty
3. Dorsey Cottage
4. Molton House

NORTH HULL STREET
5. Victorian simple Queen Anne Cottage (Roy's House)
6. Victorian Queen Anne Cottage
7. Victorian Queen Anne Cottage
7a. Victorian Queen Anne Cottage (privately owned)
8. DeWolfe-Cooper Cottage
9. Bush Cottage
10. Nall-Young House
11. Ware-Farley-Hood House
12. Cram-Lakin House
13. Graves-Haigler House
13a. Graves-Haigler House
14. Davis-Cook House
15. Mayor Reese Cottage
16. Martin-Barnes House
17. Lucas Tavern
18. Ordeman-Mitchell-Shaw House
18a. Ordeman-Mitchell-Shaw House Dependency
18b. Ordeman-Mitchell-Shaw House Barn
18c. Ordeman-Mitchell-Shaw House Washhouse
19. Campbell-Holtzclaw Cottage
20. Davis-Cook House Cookhouse
21. Thompson Mansion

WORKING BLOCK
22. Grist Mill
23. Cotton Gin
24. Drugstore Museum and Print Shop
25. Molton Outbuilding
26. Cram-Lakin Outbuilding

27. Molton Outbuilding
28. Haigler Plantation Office
29. Blacksmith Shop
30. Rose-Morris House
31. Clanton Kitchen

COLUMBUS STREET
32. Carpenter's Shop
33. Brittan-Dennis House

LIVING BLOCK
34. Adams Chapel School
35. Old Alabama Town Church
36. Corner Grocery Store
37. Log Cabin
38. Pole Barn
39. Shotgun House
40. Country Doctor's Office
41. Well/transformer Housing
42. Carriage House
43. Dogtrot
44. Grange Hall

JEFFERSON STREET
45. Gallagher House
46. Noble House

STREETS SHOWN ON MAPS
Randolph St
Columbus St
N. McDonough St
N. Hull St
Jefferson St
Madison Ave
N. Decatur St

OTHER
Kiwanis Park
Bus lane
Parking
Wells

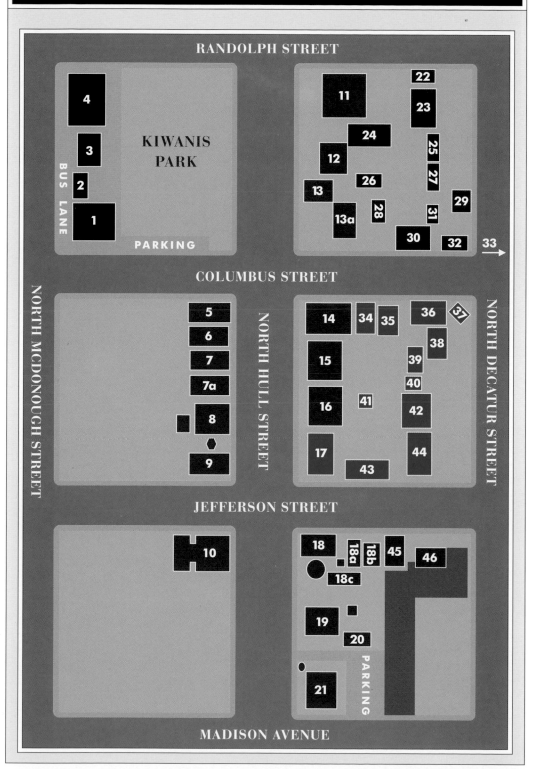

KIWANIS PARK

Your noble order never performed a more philanthropic deed than to lease the spacious Crommelin lot to be used as an ideal playground for the children of East Montgomery.
  —Mrs. Emilie Littlepage Hannon, a neighborhood resident,
    to George A. Thomas, president of Kiwanis Club, 14 February 1923

arly settler Charles Crommelin built his house on this site in the mid–nineteenth century, and in 1923 his descendants donated the property to the city for a park that the Kiwanis Club originally sponsored.

Covering more than half a city block, Kiwanis Park is an integral part of Old Alabama Town. Maintained by the city of Montgomery's Department of Parks and Recreation, it is the site of fun and exciting programs including "StoryTales" and the popular "Sounds of Summer" concerts. Throughout the year students picnic and play and visitors enjoy strolling under the trees.

Kiwanis Park offers space for many activities.

LOEB RECEPTION CENTER

301 COLUMBUS STREET

Rectangular masonry structure, flat roof, altered fenestration

The Loeb Reception Center was named for James L. Loeb, one of the founders of Landmarks Foundation, its first president, and chair of the board for fifteen years. The Foundation has it headquarters in this center, which is located on the corner of Columbus and North McDonough Streets. Here visitors can receive information, obtain tickets, and shop in the museum store. Although not a nineteenth-century building, the Center is a warm and welcoming spot which took on a new life in 1996.

Through the 1960s, North Hull Street and those bordering it became more and more commercial. It was during this time that an auto parts company constructed the warehouse structure that is now home to the Reception Center. In the early 1990s, Landmarks Foundation purchased the building, as it has other property in the vicinity. In 1995 the Board of Directors decided to renovate it for offices, a visitor center, and a museum store. Under the dynamic leadership of Board President Edith Crook and Vice President Elizabeth Mazyck, a campaign raised $500,000 for the project, and with the assistance of Mayor Emory Folmar, who supplied in-kind support, the conversion brought about a dramatic change in the former warehouse's appearance and use.

Visitors to Old Alabama Town stop first at the Reception Center where a friendly greeting welcomes them to a nineteenth-century world.

DORSEY COTTAGE SHANTY, DORSEY COTTAGE, AND SHAFFER GARDEN

Greek Revival cottage with colonnaded inset porch

amed for Thomas Dorsey, who was born 13 August 1834 in Ireland and died 15 August 1859 and who owned and lived in this cottage in the 1850s, the Dorsey Cottage is typical of many which lined Montgomery's thoroughfares. Its original site was the northeast corner of South Hull and Washington Streets. Possibly built by Thomas Dorsey, it has a hipped roof and inset col-

onnaded porch, as does the Reese Cottage across North Hull Street. On the interior, two rooms on each side flank the ubiquitous central hall which flairs at the rear, creating a fifth room. In 1999, Landmarks Foundation moved the cottage and the two-room saddlebag structure, referred to on period maps as a "shanty." This small building is the backdrop for the Shaffer Garden.

Named for Landmarks Foundation's longtime architect and friend, John Shaffer, the Shaffer Garden honors an individual who contributed years to the development of Old Alabama Town. The replicated well, pleached crape myrtles, and period plantings illustrate the way a yard of this size might have looked in nineteenth-century central Alabama.

A "saddlebag" shanty (above) provides a backdrop for Shaffer Garden in the side yard of Greek Revival Dorsey Cottage (below).

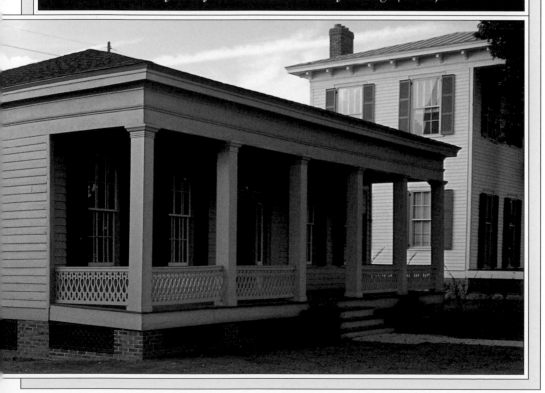

MOLTON HOUSE

The twentieth anniversary of this worthy institution [Working Woman's home] has passed. It has bravely withstood trials and hardships and stands today the leading charitable institution in the State.
—*Montgomery Advertiser*, 14 February 1901

I-house with colonnaded porch, bracketed cornices, and two rear lean-tos

 lthough built by lawyer Jefferson Franklin Jackson in 1858, this columned I-house was the home of planter Charles Molton at the time of the Civil War. Molton and his family moved into town from their plantation in the eastern part of Montgomery County in 1860. Four years later, believing that the Confederacy had a better chance of survival west of the Mississippi River, he began a move to Texas with his slaves. In Mississippi, however, federal troops stopped them and freed the slaves, forcing Molton to return to Alabama.

Before his ill-fated journey, Molton had sold his house to his sister, Narcissa, for twelve thousand dollars. Later, she rented the house: one of the tenants was E. Y. Fair, former minister to Belgium, who leased it for a year. In 1881 the Association for Aiding Working Women and the Helpless purchased it.

In line with the nation's aroused social consciousness, prominent Montgomery women realized there were many areas of need, and in this particular instance, they focused on the difficult circumstances many single women faced. Incorporated in May 1881 under the presidency of Mrs. Cornelia Bethea Graham, widow of lawyer Malcolm Daniel Graham, the Association began its work.

The Association's mission was to provide a home for single working women, primarily Caucasian domestics, and in some cases their children as well. With a matron for supervision, the home opened in the Molton House, beginning a longtime service to the community. The city's first continuous organized charity, which changed its name to the Working Woman's Home Association, gained support as local families donated funds to construct small cottages on the grounds, accompanying the two original saddlebag houses flanking the rear of the big house.

*The colonnaded front porch gives this structure, an I-house with two lean-tos,
a distinctly urban air. Dating from the late 1850s, the Molton House was the
city residence of a prosperous planter with a large family.*

Until 1992, the Association provided small one-room apartments with effi-
ciency kitchens for working and elderly women. With changing times, the organization decided to sell the property and discontinue the housing but to carry on
their philanthropic activities of aiding women and children.

Selling the property to the Alabama Hospital Association, the Working
Woman's Association, with the purchaser, offered the house to Landmarks Foundation with both contributing funds to assist with its relocation to Old Alabama
Town. The move occurred in March 1993, and in 2000 the Foundation completed the restoration.

The structure is a distinguished example of an I-house, a form that features
two rooms over two rooms separated by a central hall. One-story rear lean-tos
offer additional room; in this case there are two such appendages. Some structures of this kind are simple, while others more elaborate. With its graceful colonnade, bracketed cornice, and interior faux painting, the Molton House is a
sophisticated example of an urban I-house.

ORDEMAN-MITCHELL-SHAW HOUSE

THE ORDEMAN AND MITCHELL STORY

I will sell my brick house on the corner of Jefferson and Hull low for cash. The house is new and furnished in the best style with ten good size rooms.
—C. C. Ordeman, *Daily Advertiser and Gazette*, 18 December 1853

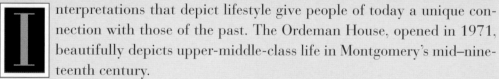

Two-story scored masonry Italianate town house with basement, bracketed cornice, and hoodmolds

I nterpretations that depict lifestyle give people of today a unique connection with those of the past. The Ordeman House, opened in 1971, beautifully depicts upper-middle-class life in Montgomery's mid–nineteenth century.

An Italianate town house on its original site, the 1850s Ordeman House represents a new era in southern architectural tastes inspired by the rampant romanticism of the era. While the town house retained a symmetrical form, the Italianate style introduced new concepts including the idea that columns were no longer essential. The more elaborate, asymmetrical Italianate villa also began making an appearance around the region, and several of these once graced Montgomery's streets.

The Ordeman-Mitchell-Shaw House, the nucleus of Old Alabama Town, was Landmarks Foundation's first restoration.

Ladies entertained their friends during "at homes," such as teas, in their formal parlors.

The Ordeman House is a somewhat austere masonry structure of brick, plastered and scored to resemble fashionable stone, with three stories, one of which is below ground level. It is a "half-house" with the rooms on the south side; the north side, maintaining symmetry, has false chimneys and windows, matching the actual ones on the south. The designer limited exterior details to an iron-railed balcony on the southern and western facades, paired brackets lining the cornice, and hoodmolds over the front windows.

An impressive collection of mid-nineteenth-century furniture, artwork, lighting devices, china, and glassware well portrays the manner and style in which one element of society passed its days at midcentury. Dominating the entrance hall is a gracefully curving staircase. On the first level, double parlors with handsome, massive window and door surrounds are welcoming guests today just as they have for the past 150 years. The lady of the house could serve her "at home" guests in the stylish front parlor, furnished in the fashionable Rococo Revival, and in the back parlor with its Empire motif, the master could challenge a friend to a game of chess.

On the second floor, the master bedroom with its high, half-tester bed is in the back of the house. Was it because the owners wanted to be away from street noises or was it so they could keep close watch on the courtyard and rear dependency buildings?

A guest room, furnished with a "button" bed, was comfortable for visitors who stayed sometimes for weeks, as travel was difficult and slow. People tried to get as much time out of a long, hard journey as possible, enjoying the pleasures of a city before setting out on the return trip. Indeed, at times this must have been trying for hosts and hostesses.

A child's room with toys and appropriate furniture and a sewing room with a mechanical sewing machine indicated two major concerns of a lady of the house—caring for children and clothing her family. In the mid–nineteenth century, motherhood was fraught with anxieties as infant mortality was high: leading causes of death included teething, spasms, worms, croup, cholera infantum, and bilious colic. There were clothing stores and professional seamstresses in

Muslin hangings on this handsome bed kept out flying insects.
(Photo courtesy Landmarks Foundation)

Outbuildings include the two-story kitchen-slave quarters building and a washhouse, the latter mandated by city ordinance in the 1850s to prevent the spreading of wash fires.

Montgomery, including the itinerant ones who would go to homes at the beginning of each season and make new wardrobes for the family. Even so, many housewives still sewed, and they must have greeted the development of the domestic sewing machine with relief and delight.

Dining rooms, one formal and one for the family, are on the lower level with windows opening onto a dry moat, an Italianate characteristic adopted by leading architects of the day. This element permitted light into a basement area, making it an integral part of the living arrangements within a house. Two storage rooms provided secure places for keeping staples, which were doled out each day by the mistress in consultation with the cook.

Domestic duties in the rear courtyard were carried out by servants who occupied the second floor of the kitchen and the quarters dependency. An original structure on the site, this masonry building is one of only three of its kind surviving in the city. Replicated "necessaries," the carriage house and washhouse, on archaeologically determined locations, depict aspects of urban life while a garden and barn denote the rural aspects still prevalent and essential at the time.

*Food preparation took place in the scullery adjacent to the
main kitchen, where most of the cooking was done. The large copper kettle
is for heating water.*

The Ordeman House was Landmarks Foundation's first restoration and remains the crown jewel of its museum buildings. Surrounding it is an air of mystery involving failed aspirations, sad losses, foreclosures, premarital agreements, and missing persons.

When Montgomery became state capital in 1846, its population increased as people saw the potential opportunities in a growing, politically and commercially significant city. Charles Ordeman, a twenty-five-year-old German immigrant who noted himself as an architect and engineer, arrived in Montgomery in 1850, an aspiring, ambitious young man in a place ripe for talents such as his.

Announcing his arrival with an ad in the *Alabama Journal* in June, he established a professional office in the heart of Montgomery near Court Square. Traveling to New York, on 5 September he married Sarah A. Bogert in Trinity Church. Two years his senior, the bride was a native New Yorker and an Episcopalian. On 23 November, Ordeman bought two lots at the corner of North Hull and Jefferson Streets, and in all probability, the Greek Revival "Campbell" cottage provided a living space for the newlyweds while Charles began the construction of the three-story Italianate town house next door.

During his first two years in Montgomery, Charles thrived, receiving public acclaim for his architectural services and obtaining contracts for the Court Street Methodist Church and the new courthouse. For investments in the Montgomery Gas Light Company and in downtown property, he mortgaged the big house under way on North Hull Street. In the fall of 1853, however, he advertised it for sale, stating that he was going to be "absent from the city," and about the same time, he sold the cottage he and Sarah occupied to a jeweler, John Campbell. Unfortunately, the big house did not sell on the market, but mortgage holders forced foreclosure and on 6 February 1854 it sold at "public outcry" for $4,160.00. Notices of the impending sale stated that the house had never been occupied.

What happened to Ordeman? Obviously talented and ambitious, did he see greener pastures elsewhere or was he running from his mounting debts? Where did he and Sarah go when they left Montgomery? Although there were no Ordeman children in the 1850 census, did they have any by the time they departed? Extensive research has failed to find answers to these varied questions, but there is always hope that some day historians will uncover the rest of the Ordeman story.

After the public sale, B. F. Noble, who lived to the east of the Ordeman House and was one of the creditors who had forced the disposal, immediately purchased the house from the high bidder. In August he sold it to Julius Caesar Bonaparte Mitchell and his wife, Rebecca, a plantation family from the Mt. Meigs area of eastern Montgomery County. Many planters had town dwellings for a variety of reasons: social activities, educational opportunities for children, religious purposes, and commercial and political contacts.

Julius Mitchell was a Georgian who had joined relatives in the Mt. Meigs area as a young man; he first married Jane Murdock, daughter of the prominent Murdock family and granddaughter of John Burch, an early settler and large property owner. Sadly, Jane did not live long and Julius then courted her sister, Rebecca Ellen; however, before their marriage Sarah Murdock, the widowed mother of the two girls, required the couple to sign a prenuptial agreement. Julius thus became trustee of Rebecca's estate consisting of a half section of land and twelve slaves, agreeing that he would reserve any funds from these for Rebecca's exclusive use. They married on 17 October 1846, the day after signing the agreement.

The Mitchells had two children, Murdock and Posey, when the family purchased the house in town. In 1855, they had another daughter, Lilly.

For four years, the family owned the town house, and at the same time, Julius continued to expand his planting operations in Mt. Meigs. Though they sold the town house to druggist Erastus Jones in 1858 and lived in the country for the rest of their lives, they maintained ties in town. Rebecca was a member of St. John's Episcopal Church, and Julius became quite involved in the political activities that led up to the Civil War.

Attending the 1860 Democratic Convention in Charleston, Mitchell was with his friend William Lowndes Yancey when the latter led southern delegates out, breaking up the national party and assuring the election of Abraham Lincoln. During the Civil War, Julius organized the Thirty-fourth Alabama Infantry and served for much of the war as its colonel. Rebecca, too, gave her support to the cause, outfitting a battalion from Roanoke, Alabama, and actively participating in the Mt. Meigs Ladies Aid Society.

Mitchell returned after the war to a different world than he had known before and, along with thousands of other southerners, faced often overwhelming financial difficulties. Borrowing heavily on his land and cotton crops, he struggled to carry on his farming operations. By early 1868, he was in serious difficulties, and to add to his woes, an appraisal of his position concluded that he owed his wife's estate $51,580.00 because of his use of her property over the years. His mother-in-law, Sarah Murdock, was now to be the overseer of Rebecca's interests, and to settle the debt, Julius deeded almost everything he owned to Rebecca's estate.

Again there are unanswered questions. Had Sarah Murdock lost all faith in Julius and his abilities to manage affairs, or was this to protect the whole family if creditors came calling? There is probably no answer to that enigma, and under the circumstances either would have had been valid.

In April 1869 another crushing event occurred when nineteen-year-old Murdock died. In October, Julius followed him to the grave. Both girls married, Lilly to Thomas Barnett and Posey to Dr. C. L. Pinkston. Rebecca lived in the country until her death in 1881.

In addition to the druggist Erastus Jones, other nineteenth-century owners of the house included book dealer Joel White, but in 1905 lumberman Bruce Shaw acquired the property. His daughter, Maude, occupied the house until its purchase by the city of Montgomery and Landmarks Foundation in 1967 for its development as a house museum depicting life in 1850s Montgomery.

Landmarks conducted meticulous research for the restoration, furnishing, and interpretation of the Ordeman House, including extensive archaeology and paint analysis. The nucleus of Old Alabama Town, the house is a highly respected representative of its era and continues to attract visitors from around the world.

THE LIVING BLOCK

E nter the Living Block through a weathered picket gate, set in a fence patterned after one in rural Dallas County, Alabama. A friendly welcome awaits as you enter Lucas Tavern where your adventure begins with a tour of that historic building and its role in the busy life along the Federal Road.

Remember that for you, as for thousands of earlier travelers, this tavern was a stopping place for information and sustenance before advancing into what was frequently a vast unknown. We have made it a bit easier for you as there is the warm, southern, recorded voice of Kathryn Tucker Windham to take you further into the nineteenth century. So with Alabama's foremost storyteller as your companion on tape, discover how people once lived in this region. (The tavern keeper will give you a cassette player and all necessary instructions.)

In this block are both urban and rural structures, straightforward buildings with no pretenses, where people gathered together to satisfy various basic needs, longings, and aspirations. The houses, tavern, Grange Hall, doctor's office, store, school, church, and dependencies were a part of the fabric of nineteenth-century life.

In addition to the buildings, there are other elements to help tell the story. Swept backyards to keep brush fires and snakes away from dwellings and scuppernong arbors for fruit and shade were in most rural and even in many urban areas. Beyond these

amenities and the Yancey Dogtrot, meander along a winding lane, stopping to visit the sites and keeping an eye out for surprises along the way.

During the spring, old roses bloom along the paths and around the doorways of the Old Alabama Town buildings. Other period plantings include iris, day lilies, althea, crape and wax myrtles, and red cedars. Indigenous trees such as sycamore, magnolia, various oaks, tulip poplar, sweet gum, and hickory shade the lane and buildings, giving protection from the southern sun.

A very special tree, the Chinaberry, was an eighteenth-century import from Asia. Known also as the Pride of China, it won favor in the eyes of many, including Thomas Jefferson who planted them at his home, Monticello. In the 1820s, this hardy, popular tree lined the streets of Montgomery as the new town attempted a bit of beautification. It spread prolifically throughout the southern

Old Alabama Town Herb Society tends the garden designed and initiated by Judy Youngblood.

countryside and grew in the yards of both rich and poor. A Chinaberry tree stands by the log cabin, a relic of a practical and ornamental plant that has lost the position it once enjoyed.

A hitching rail by the Grange Hall and large iron watering troughs at the carriage house and store illustrate the importance of animals as means of moving people and goods from one place to another. In front of the school, an old water pump provided cool water to students and teachers on hot and dusty days. There, too, hangs a school bell to summon children to their lessons. A red fireplug in front of the grocery store stood ready to provide water for volunteer firemen to use in protecting the town.

The herb garden is an aromatic must. Planted by volunteer Judy Youngblood, it is now under the care of the Old Alabama Town Herb Society. The handsome iron fence surrounding it is from Dallas County.

Two large iron pots in the log cabin yard are reminders of hard work. Women washed clothes in the deeper pot while in the other, wider and shallower, men made syrup, often the only sweetener folks had and a great treat for hot biscuits when flour was on hand.

As you return to Lucas Tavern note the replica of the well house on the green. Based on similar structures such as milk houses, springhouses, and outhouses, this handsome structure discretely covers an electrical transformer (map 41).

MAP 17　　　　　　　THE LIVING BLOCK　　　　　　　25

LUCAS TAVERN

The Subscriber has taken over that well-known stand on Line Creek formerly operated by James Abercrombie.
　—W. B. Lucas, *Montgomery Republican*, 6 January 1821

Four-room frame building with enclosed central hall; small stoops, front and back

L ucas Tavern and the Federal Road played significant roles in the story of western expansion and the movement of people into the lower South, the southwest of the early nineteenth century. When the United States government acquired the Louisiana Territory in 1803, it quickly realized the need for reliable means of communication with New Orleans. Surveys and treaties with various Indian tribes resulted in the development of two systems of roads: the Natchez Trace and the Federal Road. The latter extended from Milledgeville, then capital of Georgia, to St. Stephens on the Tombigbee River in southwest Alabama. There it linked with roads to New Orleans.

After the opening of the Alabama Territory for settlement, the Federal Road, winding its way through the Creek Nation and then into the heartland of Alabama, became more heavily traveled as settlers hurried to lay claim to the newly available lands. Located every fifteen or so miles along the rough and hazardous thoroughfare were

Lucas Tavern's inviting dining room once hosted such dignitaries as the Marquis de La Fayette.

"stands," or taverns providing food, drink, shelter, and information. While some had unsavory reputations, one of the most acclaimed was Lucas Tavern, located at Line Creek, a community just inside the Alabama boundary.

Originally James Abercrombie operated the tavern, a two-room open dogtrot, but in 1820 Walter and Eliza Lucas took over its management. Walter was a land agent for the Alabama Company, the Georgian developers of East Alabama Town. First cousins, both he and Eliza had grown up in the Milledgeville area and were members of a family that had come down from Virginia. A veteran of the Creek-American conflicts of the War of 1812, Walter had been at the Battle of Calabee Creek where Eliza's first husband, Sam Butts, had died. This event had occurred just a few miles east of where the town of Line Creek later developed.

Walter Lucas was a citizen of some standing in East Alabama Town with a store on Commerce Street and a pole boat, the *Eliza*, which plied the Alabama River to Mobile and back. He was instrumental in the incorporation of his village and that of New Philadelphia, forming the town of Montgomery. In

This 1940s photograph depicts Lucas Tavern on its original site in eastern Montgomery County. The porch was not an original element, so renovation architects decided not to replace it. (Photo courtesy Landmarks Foundation)

Restored at the corner of North Hull and Jefferson Streets, Lucas Tavern is the entrance to Old Alabama Town's Living Block.

fact, he received the credit for suggesting the name in honor of General Richard Montgomery.

Although well established in town, late in 1820 the couple moved to Line Creek with the announcement of their taking over the tavern appearing in the first issue of the *Montgomery Republican*, 6 January 1821:

> *The subscriber has taken over that well-known stand on Line Creek, Alabama, formerly occupied by James Abercrombie, Esq., where he intends to devote his attention to the comfort and satisfaction of those who favor him with their patronage. He also continues his mercantile business at Montgomery, Alabama and has on hand a very general assortment of Dry Goods hardware, Cutlery, and Groceries all of which will be sold low for Lucas's bills or other money only. W. B. Lucas*

Walter also had a store and gin in Line Creek, but continued his operations in Montgomery. Day-to-day tavern activities were the responsibility of Eliza.

Modifications to the building took place about this time with the enclosure of the dogtrot and the addition of two smaller, lean-to rooms. One of these, for dining, had a stylish chair rail and a door leading to the outside kitchen.

Simple and functional, Lucas Tavern served an important role with its innkeepers being both repositories and dispensers of information on the road, its condition, and the situation within the state and the Creek Nation. Many travelers availed themselves of their hospitality, and in 1825, the Lucases hosted their most distinguished guest, the Marquis de La Fayette, on his grand tour of the United States.

Invited by the United States as a "Guest of the Nation," La Fayette, revered for the help he gave to the strug-

Playing cards helped travelers relax after their journeys.

gling colonies in the Revolutionary War, arrived in this country in August 1824. After being lavishly entertained throughout the East, he left Washington in February 1825 for a trip through all of the states. Arriving in Alabama several days behind schedule, he and his companions unexpectedly spent the night at Lucas Tavern as they made their way to Montgomery.

Thomas Woodward, among the volunteer Alabama militia accompanying La Fayette, wrote, "That night we reached Walter B. Lucas. Everything was 'done up' better than it will ever be again; one thing only was lacking—time—we could not stay long enough." Eliza was probably glad to see the entourage on the road early the next morning.

Five years later, another adventurer on the Federal Road, the Scottish lawyer James Stuart, did record a menu and a descriptive account of his stop at "Mrs. Lucas' hotel" where he found an excellent meal of "chicken pie, ham, vegetables, pudding and pies, . . . so well put upon the table, so well cooked, and the dessert, consisting of dried fruits, preserved strawberries and plums, was so excellent, and withal the guests seemed to be made so welcome to everything that was best. . . . The preserved plum was in . . . great perfection here. There was wine on the table, as well as brandy and water; and plenty of time was allowed us to partake of our repast. The whole charge was only three-quarters of a dollar for each person." He also noted that Mrs. Lucas was "the fattest woman he had ever seen for her age [thirty-five]." Did Eliza mislead him, taking the woman's prerogative of fibbing about the years already spent on earth? Born about 1791, she married Sam Butts in 1807 and in 1830 would have been closer to forty than thirty-five. Stuart commented on how well Mrs. Lucas managed her affairs and that she sat at the head of the table with her husband sitting to her right. His closing remarks were "this certainly was as comfortable meal as we found anywhere in travelling in the United States." Obviously, Eliza was a successful businesswoman and a cook who from all appearances thoroughly enjoyed her own cooking.

In 1842, the Lucases, caught up again in the westward movement, moved to Noxubee County, Mississippi. On 26 August 1843, Eliza, suffering from an unidentified illness, died in the neighboring town of Louisville, having gone there for treatment at nearby Winston Springs. On 20 September 1843 the *Alabama Journal* carried an obituary from the *Mississippi Independent*: "a link is thus broken which connected a chain of relationship through three states, and this sad memorial will moisten many a distant eye and heave many an aching bosom." The 1860 census listed Walter as a farmer living in Noxubee County with a prospering Walter Jr. classified as a planter. On 26 October 1862 Walter died in Louisville but there are no details on his death.

By the time the Lucases left Alabama, many other roads were open, and the Federal Road had much less use. The old tavern became a residence and in the 1930s was in a dilapidated condition when the Daughters of the American Revolution placed a historic marker commemorating La Fayette's visit. Later, the venerable building served as a storage place for cattle feed, but many remembered its role, and in 1978, owners Stewart Fuzzell and Vergie Broward gave the building to Landmarks Foundation to move to Old Alabama Town.

At the completion of its restoration in January 1980, the building became headquarters and reception center for Landmarks Foundation until the fall of 1996. Today, Old Alabama Town interprets it as a stop for weary travelers along the Federal Road, telling the story of the Lucas family and their era. As the oldest building remaining in Montgomery County, it serves as an important reminder of Alabama's place in the country's westward expansion movement.

DOGTROT

Houses . . . are built double, a set of rooms on each side of a wide passage, which is floored and ceiled in common with the rest of the house, but is entirely open at each end, being unfurnished with either gate or door, and forming a thoroughfare for the family through the house. . . . When the air within the house is close and sultry, almost to suffocation, and the unmerciful rays of the sun without glare upon the head beyond endurance, it is a pleasant relief to sit in these halls beneath the shade, where too there is a current of air whenever there is a breath stirring. Here the southern planter loves to sit, or to lie stretched at full length.

—Philip Henry Gosse, *Letters from Alabama*

Two-room frame building with open central porch

lthough Gosse beautifully described the dogtrot house, what he did not tell was the origin of its vernacular name. The open passageway, in addition to providing a "thoroughfare for the family," was also a means by which the dogs moved through as well.

First-generation dogtrots were log, evolving from one-pen (room) log cabins when the occupant needed more space. By adding another room of the same size and connecting the two by the passage, the family more than doubled its home. A practical type, well suited to a hot clime, the dogtrot became a fixture on the southern landscape.

Old Alabama Town has two open-dogtrot houses—one a simple two-room structure and the other a more complex I-house with a dogtrot hallway. Although not obvious from the exterior, many other structures here are essentially

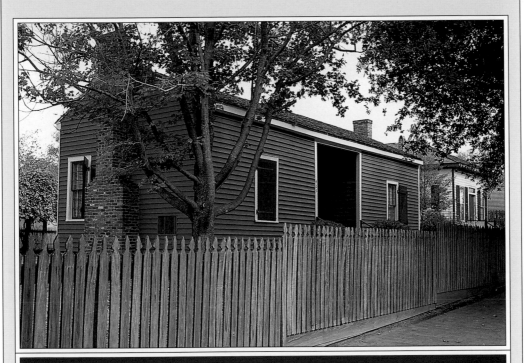

Above: Moved and restored, the dogtrot house serves as staff offices in Old Alabama Town. Opposite page: This 1890s photograph of the dogtrot house notes that lawyer, orator, and secessionist William Lowndes Yancey spent his last days here. It stood on his plantation north of Montgomery on the Wetumpka Road. Yancey died in the house in July 1863. (Photo courtesy Landmarks Foundation)

dogtrots, because the central hall plan, refined and enclosed, prevailed in most southern houses until the 1850s for much the same reason. With the doors open, breezes moved throughout the house, bringing welcome relief from summer's heat.

The two-room dogtrot stood on the plantation purchased by Montgomery lawyer and ardent secessionist William Lowndes Yancey in 1859. Yancey died of kidney disease in this house in 1863.

Owners in the early years of the twentieth century greatly altered the appearance of the structure, but although obscured, the old dogtrot survived. In May 1979, Landmarks Foundation removed all additions and relocated the original building to Old Alabama Town for preservation because it is one of the few surviving houses of a style that once provided shelter for thousands.

GRANGE HALL

Something to eat must be our first thought . . . [with cotton] a secondary consideration.
    —Resolutions of Greene County Grange, December 1873

The plan of the house should be that lain down in the ritual of subordinate Granges to be of such dimensions as decided by the Granges.
    —F. M. Tankersley, Secretary, Log of Pintlala Grange, No. 175, October 1873

Frame building with one large room and an anteroom; small stoops on west and south facades

ollowing a tour of the country in 1867, Oliver Kelly, a clerk in the U.S. Department of Agriculture, founded the Grange. Its multiple purposes included economic, social, and cultural improvement for farmers and their families with agricultural interests of foremost importance. Crop diversification and soil conservation received prime consideration, but business matters such as money lending, insurance, and cooperatives also had important roles.

In the years following the Civil War, citizens of Pintlala, a rural community in the southern part of Montgomery County, struggled with the changed economic and social systems. They, with farmers throughout the South, sought ways to deal with recurring agricultural crises, and in hopes of solutions, they organized a local chapter of the National Grange of the Patrons of Husbandry. In 1874, they built a Grange Hall in accordance with national specifications.

On 15 November 1873 the *Alabama Beacon*, a west Alabama newspaper, reported that there were 109 subordinate Granges in the state, and on 27 November 1873 delegates met in Montgomery and established a State Grange whose membership in 1874 reached 650 chapters.

Resolutions from one in the western part of the state indicated the major concerns and purposes of the movement: that emphasis should be placed on foodstuffs and not on cotton. The Dallas-Autauga-Prattville Grange urged greater attention to the raising of stock, corn, peas, potatoes, and grains and an early

Once the meeting house of the Pintlala Chapter of the National Grange for the Patrons of Husbandry, the Grange Hall now serves as a classroom and an exhibit area in Old Alabama Town's Living Block.

return to the cash system. Most chapters took strong stands for money wages and uniform contracts with labor and vigorously protested the crop-lien system that tied farmers to planting cotton—the cash crop.

Although the Grange urged diversification, most members had to deal with the reality of cotton as a cash crop, one which they could not afford to overlook. Neither could they ignore sharecropping that was providing means of survival to both blacks and whites. There was such a lack of available cash throughout the South that supporting a purely wage system of farming was impossible.

From its organization in 1873, the Pintlala Grange followed the path of others and throughout the next twenty years welcomed men and women into membership; in fact, the Grange was one of the first national groups, with the exception of churches and social clubs, to have women as individual members. The rolls note "farmer's wife," "teacher," and "farmer's daughter." The meetings, conducted according to certain rules and rites, focused on programs designed to inform and to bring people together. There were frequent picnics, dinners, and singings; the Pintlala inventories list paraphernalia for rituals and utensils for social affairs.

The Grange did not, theoretically, have a political agenda, but its members did hold public office and there was cooperation between it and the Farmers Alliance on certain issues. Failing to solve the many agricultural problems, by the 1890s the Grange was all but dead; however, it had paved the way for the Alliance, the Farmers' Wheel, and the Populist Party movement in Alabama.

The last state meeting of the Grange took place in the Pintlala Grange Hall in 1892, but the building's agricultural usefulness did not end there. In 1917 the Federal Land Bank Association organized as the National Farm Loan Association of Pintlala whose members consisted of borrowers on farm property in Montgomery, Lowndes, and Crenshaw Counties under the provisions of the Federal Land Loan Act. Meetings of this group, which became the Alabama Farm Bureau, continued for several years in Pintlala, thus giving the Grange Hall another distinction in agricultural history.

The Grange Hall was also the school, and until 1922, the building served as the elementary facility for the area. Later it was a residence, the community library, and a meeting place for Boy Scouts and other groups; several people remembered going to square dances there during the 1920s. In the late 1970s, the Board of Education gave the by then abandoned structure to Landmarks Foundation which brought it to Old Alabama Town. Restored, it has a vital role as Grange Hall School, a specialized program for elementary classes.

This building in many ways exemplifies the agricultural dilemmas faced by southern farmers attempting to cope with the new order in the post–Civil War era. The Grange was perhaps most beneficial because of its focus on educational and social goals and in proving that farmers could work together for the common good.

CARRIAGE HOUSE

As my business requires my continual absence from Montgomery, I have concluded to sell my residence. It is built of brick and stucco; containing eight large, comfortable rooms, together with every necessary and convenient outbuilding—stable, carriage house, etc.
  —Samuel Swan, *Confederation*, 31 May 1858

1 Rockaway and harness; 1 large Phaeton Carriage; 1 buggy and harness.
  —Estate Papers of J. J. Seibels, 24 August 1866

Two-story board with beaded battens Italianate building; bracketed cornice; wide double doors; arched and louvered windows

Samuel Swan, a native of Massachusetts, was one of the opportunists who came to Montgomery at the time the town became the state capital. With entrepreneurial spirit, he established a jewelry business, a newspaper, and conducted lotteries in Alabama and Georgia. In 1858, he left Montgomery to study homeopathic medicine in Wilmington, Delaware.

Swan sold his fine home and its outbuildings to businessman and newspaper publisher John Jacob Seibels in July 1858 for twenty thousand dollars. Situated on a commanding position at the crest of the South Hull Street hill, the house, three years old when Swan sold it, became known as the Seibels-Ball-Lanier House, descending through the daughters of the Seibels family until 1955. One of the Italianate villas for which Montgomery became justly renowned, it helped usher in a transformation in architecture as fashion moved from the earlier boxy symmetrical Greek Revival to the asymmetrical style that gained favor at midcentury. Sadly, this house did not survive.

The carriage house, although symmetrical in shape, bears witness to the period's fascination with Italianate adornment and was perhaps even more elegant for its purposes than the main house. Sporting a low hip roof with a cornice dripping with brackets on all elevations, the building proclaims its presence aided by the original colors: rich chocolate brown with pistachio-green trim. The board and beaded battens add other handsome, decorative touches. On the interior, the exposed mortise and tenon construction (pegged) demonstrates an ancient method. The floor boards, more than twelve inches wide, would quite adequately have supported the weight of the carriage and buggies.

A South Carolinian, J. J. Seibels had wealth and position. Appointed minister to Belgium by Franklin Pierce, he served from 1853 to 1855 and upon returning home continued his career as a planter, businessman, and newspaperman. He expressed his opposition to secession in the *Confederation* and other Montgomery publications, supporting the candidate of the national Democratic ticket, Stephen A. Douglas, in the election of 1860. However, upon the organization of the Confederacy, Seibels gave his support to the new government and fought in several battles with the Sixth Alabama Regiment.

When Douglas visited Montgomery early in November 1860 as election campaigning drew to a close, Seibels was his host, and when belligerent crowds threw stones at the carriage in which Douglas was riding to a rally, it could well have been the large phaeton, a light carriage with two seats facing forward, listed in Seibels's estate papers. The carriage house afforded secure, dry quarters for the carriage and other equipment, and there were also stalls for horses and the upstairs sheltered hay, feed, and extra harnesses. Stable boys and drivers spent long hours feeding and grooming the horses and polishing the vehicles which rolled out of the magnificent structure.

In 1955, the family sold the property to the Scottish Rites Masonic Order which in the 1980s donated the carriage house to Landmarks Foundation. With monetary support from the Junior League Sustainers, the Foundation moved

For more than one hundred years, this fine carriage house stood in the yard of the elegant Italianate house occupied by three prominent and related families, the Seibels, Balls, and Laniers. Through a grant from the Junior League Sustainers, Landmarks moved it to Old Alabama Town in the early 1980s.

the carriage house to Old Alabama Town in 1981 for restoration. Chemical analysis determined the original paint colors which make as vibrant a statement today as they did in the nineteenth century. The carriage dates from the turn of the century and belonged to L. B. Whitfield, a local manufacturer of the famous Alaga syrup and Whitfield pickles.

Later sale of the main house resulted in its demolition, although Landmarks Foundation and others made valiant efforts to save it.

COUNTRY DOCTOR'S OFFICE

Dr. Duncan;

My mother is suffering very much with her hip. Please send her some of those powders that you usually give her for the pain. Also send the tonic—an acid for her liver. And the Belladonna liniment that you prepared for her.

Respectfully,

L. Willingham, March 6, 1894

One-room frame structure with pedimented inset porch

homas David Duncan, a native of the small farming community of Fleta in the southern part of Montgomery County, first taught school and then attended the Medical College of Alabama in Mobile from 1889 until his graduation in 1892. Returning to his rural home, he set up practice in a small building in his parents' yard from which he practiced until his death in 1938.

Dr. Duncan's office provided a place for him to mix medicines, and his cabinets housed instruments both delicate and sharp. He visited patients on horseback, by horse and buggy, and finally by automobile. He was the epitome of the country doctor: he stayed up all night with women in labor, held the hand of the youth dying of typhoid fever, and rejoiced with the parents of children who survived whooping cough.

Life was hard at the end of the nineteenth century and into the twentieth. Most rural folk were sharecroppers, moving through life with the barest of necessities, and even though medicine was making great strides, there were diseases ravaging the lands, mercilessly debilitating the poor and showing little regard for those in better circumstances. Among those ailments that rendered such pain and despair were bilious fevers such as malaria and, as late as 1897, yellow fever. Rickets, scurvy, pellagra, and other nutritional diseases rendered many Alabamians incapable of tending crops and providing adequate food for

Dr. Duncan practiced medicine from this small office in rural Montgomery County for more than forty-five years. Exemplifying the legendary country physician, he traveled to his patients' homes by horse, buggy, and, finally, automobile.

their families, sometimes bringing wrath down upon southerners as shiftless and lazy. As late as World War I, 54 percent of Alabama boys tested for the draft had hookworm. Dr. Duncan had to face these trials in addition to various wounds, broken limbs, and contagious diseases such as diphtheria and measles.

An 1888 letter from Strata, a neighboring community, illustrates the afflictions faced by families:

I will write to you to let you hear of the death of our little Claud. He died today was a week ago. He had been sick a month but was taken serious last Sunday evening . . . with congestion of the brain. . . . Eugenia has been sick two months but she had got able to go to the garden till last monday she was taken worse. . . . Ethel has sore eyes real bad. . . . Uncle Jim suffers a great deal with risens. . . . Callie, his baby, has them on her face and head . . . Billie's baby cannot walk. he is sixteen months old.

From your cousin,

Fannie Williamson, July 14, 1888

The good doctor also on occasion had to minister to various toothaches, sending the most severe on to Montgomery as he did patients requiring major surgery. Within a farming area a man's animals were of paramount importance and at times Dr. Duncan, who also raised horses and had a dairy farm, doctored neighbors' livestock and house pets.

Physician, pharmacist, dentist, and veterinarian, Dr. Duncan and his compatriots fulfilled vital roles in their rural environment. In addition to his medical interests, Duncan also had agricultural and civic concerns, serving on the Board of Revenue and encouraging small farmers to own and occupy their own farmsteads.

This small doctor's office witnessed scenes of joy and despair, as did the physicians who attended births and deaths throughout the countryside of Alabama, ministering to all segments of the population with compassion and varying degrees of skills and knowledge. They accepted payment in whatever their patients were able to give, from eggs to loads of corn and wood. Their rewards often were just handshakes and promises as their grateful clientele struggled with circumstances far beyond their capabilities to control. Everyone looked to the doctors for wisdom, guidance, and healing.

Landmarks Foundation learned of Dr. Duncan's office from Ethel Tankersley Todd, the daughter of a rural doctor in the neighboring community of Hope Hull. With her help and that of Dr. Duncan's daughters and nephews and the Montgomery Medical Auxiliary, the Foundation moved and restored the building. The furnishings are those of Dr. Duncan, Dr. William Tankersley, and other members of the medical community. The Old Alabama Town staff has often heard stories of Dr. Duncan's contributions as friend and physician from his former patients who come by to see the office they remember from their past.

MAP 39   THE LIVING BLOCK   41

SHOTGUN HOUSE

I once asked a group of black women to define a shotgun house. After a few moments of deliberation their collective reply was: "[. . .] A house without privacy."
—John Michael Vlach, *The Afro-American Tradition in Decorative Arts*

Frame building with two abutting rooms; entrances on narrow sides with front porch and rear stoop

oved into Old Alabama Town in 1977 from its original location (the 500 block of Bainbridge Street near downtown Montgomery), this shotgun house, former home of Grant and Vinie Fitzpatrick, incorporates both personal and architectural histories.

A significant structure in the history of southern housing, shotguns such as this answered the need for economical homes, particularly in urban areas in the late nineteenth century.

The front room of the shotgun often functioned as both a bedroom and a parlor.

Anthropologists and archaeologists believe that the "shotgun" form evolved from a Nigerian house style brought to Haiti by slaves. With rooms abutting each other and no central hall, the African version had the door on the long side. After the Haitian revolution at the end of the eighteenth century, thousands of refugees descended on coastal southern cities. Bringing their architectural knowledge with them, the immigrants introduced the shotgun house to the United States.

With the doors in the gable ends, the small houses proved ideal and very practical for urban areas, fitting nicely on long, narrow lots whose front widths deter-

mined their price. Another important characteristic of the style was that owners could append room after room to the rear until the structure sometimes stretched from front to back property lines.

The exodus of former slaves from plantations into towns and cities after the Civil War created serious housing problems. Shotgun houses offered a sensible, economic solution, and soon block after block of the sturdy little buildings appeared in Montgomery and around the state. Moses Brothers Banking and Realty Company built many, and when that firm went bankrupt in the early 1890s, its holdings, including this house, went on the market.

A black man, Willis Willingham, purchased two shotgun houses on Bainbridge Street, two blocks east of this site. Occupying one, he rented the other to the Fitzpatricks. Vinie Fitzpatrick engaged in a common occupation of the day: she was a washwoman. Grant Fitzpatrick worked on the railroad, for the cotton seed oil mill, and for the ice plant.

Landmarks Foundation, with the help of the Black Culture Preservation Committee under the leadership of Dr. Zelia Evans, moved and furnished this house and restored it to its original appearance. The newspaper on the wall kept out drafts, and the equipment for washing and ironing are suggestive of Vinie Fitzpatrick's long days of work. The furniture, bedding, and room arrangements further illustrate the lifestyle of many late-nineteenth-century urban dwellers who had little, if any, privacy.

A question frequently asked deals with the origin of the term "shotgun." There are several possible answers, but the most popular is that if someone fired a shotgun from the street the shot would pepper through every room in the house.

CORNER GROCERY STORE

My grandfather rose early, 5 A.M., in order to open the store. . . . The store was open until well after dark—as late as 8 or 9 o'clock during the summer. . . . It was work for seven long days a week, 52 weeks a year.
—Granddaughter of Alex and Lena Cassimus to Landmarks Foundation, 1983

Two-room frame building with wrapped porch

n many urban neighborhoods there were corner groceries that supplied basic needs and provided gathering spots for the exchange of local gossip and world news. They were integral parts of the social and economic fabric of their communities.

This store, built in 1892 as Daniel O'Leary's Grocery and Saloon, stood at the intersection of Clay and Dickinson Streets to the west of downtown Montgomery in a stable, working-class neighborhood. At sometime in its history, a proprietor discontinued the colorful saloon aspect of the operations. In 1924, Alex Cassimus, whose grandfather had been the first Greek in Montgomery, became owner. He and his wife, Lena, operated the store until it closed in 1967.

Adjacent to the building and connected to it by a small hall was the home of the storekeeper thus making him available at all hours for his customers. The proprietorship brought with it many duties and responsibilities, not only for Mr. Cassimus but for his wife and family as well. The Cassimus granddaughter remembered: "My grandmother took over whenever my grandfather had business to attend to, eat his meals or was otherwise away from the store. There was no 'hired help,' no days off (not even Sunday) and certainly no vacations."

A back room, through which the family entered from the house next door, offered them a place to spend some time together where the wife could watch both the children and the store. It was also the area in which the storekeeper could retreat on occasions to take care of his financial affairs and consider how to collect from his neighbors and friends—not an easy task in many instances.

Sheltering the facade of the building, a wide roof offered a cool porch "with three upright posts and two vertical planks for people to sit and 'chew the fat.' This was really a neighborhood gathering place for men. I can still see my grandfather sitting on the store steps, solving the world's problems with several other men seated on the benches."

On the side of the store, the wide delivery doors witnessed the arrival of fresh country produce, piece goods, coffee and other staples, miscellaneous items including thread, scissors, tablets, pencils and one-cent candies and cookies, "dear to a child's heart and stomach."

The house in which the family lived is now in the Cottage Hill Historic District, having been taken there in 1982. Privately moved and restored, it stands in the period neighborhood within a few blocks of its original site. The store opened in Old Alabama Town in July 1983. It is a reminder of the many similar corner groceries that provided sustenance and companionship to people throughout Alabama and the nation.

This small store, and many like it, were essential to the economic and social well-being of the community

OLD ALABAMA TOWN CHURCH

We have purchased a lot, erected a building, and paid for it, that our colored Sabbath School of 45 and its Negro church may soon be organized into a separate church.
    —Minutes of the Session, First Presbyterian Church, 1885

One-story frame building with long windows, cornice molding and small steeple

From the founding of Montgomery's First Presbyterian Church in 1824, whites and blacks had worshiped together with the latter sitting in a gallery reserved for them. However, in the early 1880s, the African-American members requested a separate congregation which precipitated the construction of a church at the corner of Stone Street and Cleveland Avenue. Late in 1885 the writer of the Minutes of the Session reflected on the church building as being of "good style and comfortably furnished."

Although it was a simple one-room edifice, the new church did have a number of notable architectural features including long windows shielded by louvered shutters and handsome cornice moldings.

For several years, the white church kept close watch on the newer one, hiring black ministers to preach. In 1888, however, at the request of the new congregation, the Session voted to "dismiss from this church the colored members that they might organize a church of their own officers and under the name of the First Presbyterian Colored Church of Montgomery."

In 1966 the black Central Alabama Presbytery dissolved, and the East Alabama Presbytery received the Cleveland Avenue Presbyterian Church under its jurisdiction. The Session then asked the Presbytery's Church Extension Committee's assistance in purchasing or building a new church as I-85 was beginning its path through Montgomery with a bridge passing almost directly

Left: Originally named First Colored Presbyterian Church, this building served its congregation on the corner of Stone Street and Cleveland Avenue until the interstate plowed through Montgomery in the 1960s. Above: Antique pews provide upright seating for the activities that go on in the church. (Courtesy Landmarks Foundation)

over the Cleveland Avenue site. The congregation acquired a sanctuary at the corner of Goode and Wade Streets and renamed itself the Calvary Presbyterian Church. Dedication services took place on 19 January 1969.

Landmarks Foundation with the help of the Black Culture Preservation Committee, under the guidance of Dr. Zelia Evans, moved the church to Old Alabama Town for preservation. Needing old pews, the Foundation traded the modern ones then in the building for the present seats which originally served a small country congregation in a neighboring county.

On 4 December 1977, the Foundation dedicated the restored church citing its architectural and historical significance within the community. It continues to play a vital role within Old Alabama Town, symbolic of the religious life of this region.

ADAMS CHAPEL SCHOOL

One of the first students was Adelia Adams [who] many years later recalled going to school to Uncle Reid and thrilling to the magic of learning to read and write and do my numbers.
—L. H. Adams Jr. "Adams Chapel School"

One-room frame structure with front and side entrances

A prolific family, the Adamses lived and farmed in the southwestern part of Alabama's Barbour County during a time when public education in rural areas was almost nonexistent. A clan with many branches, each with children, the Adamses took it upon themselves to provide for the religious training and schooling of their broods.

In 1895 Fabian Adams deeded land to the Methodist Church and with his brothers, sons, and nephews constructed a small wooden building, Adams Chapel, which at first also doubled as a school. It was soon evident that this was not adequate and in 1898 the family built a one-room school across the road that they named Adams Chapel School.

In 1900 Alabama, the average school year was sixty-two to sixty-eight days. Scheduled around the farming cycle, school opened in late October or November, after the harvest, and closed in time for spring planting. Teacher salaries ranged from $18 to $25 a month; the state expenditure for each student was $1.44.

Built to the specifications of the State Board of Education, the simple gabled Adams Chapel School has a series of windows on the west side to provide proper lighting in an area with no electricity. With students facing north and academia discouraging the use of the left hand, there were no shadows cast upon their writing. Set on cypress stumps, the sturdy building withstood the ravages of storm, drought, and hundreds of children during the fifty years it was the education center for the communities of Texasville and Edgefield.

Although a college education was not necessary for a teacher, local school boards administered examinations to determine applicants' qualifications. Alpheus

Moved to Old Alabama Town in 1982, Adams Chapel School represents the one-room schools that once provided Alabama's children with a basic education.

Reid Adams, passing the test with high marks, was the first teacher as well as a member of the sponsoring family. Over the next half century, a number of Adamses taught in this classroom as did other individuals. Many of the teachers were students from Troy State Teachers College who would work a year, go to school a year, and so on until they had completed their studies.

The 1930 student body gathers for an important photograph with the school mascot in attendance.

Students from the first through the seventh grade attended Adams Chapel School. Utilizing the universally revered McGuffey Readers and Blue Back Spellers, teachers faced the responsibilities of preparing several lesson plans for each of the seven grades every day. In a situation such as this, it was necessary for the older pupils to help teach the younger.

Students had to perform other duties in addition to their scholastic efforts. Older boys kept the woodstove warm and filled the water bucket while girls swept and dusted the room, keeping the rows of desks twenty-four inches apart as required by state law. Desks were the property of the students, and children had to bring larger ones as they grew.

The state, working to improve its educational standards and facilities, closed this small school in 1948 and sent the students to a county consolidated facility. Poetically, the last teacher was also an Adams.

Members of the Adams family knew of Old Alabama Town and its need for a one-room school and relayed information to Landmarks about the Adams Chapel School which a former student, Colin Hartzog, had rescued, moving it to his farm as a storage shed. At first reluctant to part with it, the peanut farmer finally agreed to the building's removal to Montgomery. It arrived in Old Alabama Town in September 1982, and one year later, on 9 October 1983, large numbers of the Adams family and the general public attended its dedication.

During its restoration, Landmarks Foundation had a color analyst examine the structure. Expecting the exterior to be red, it was a distinct shock when the report came back denoting green as the original color. Although failing to be the anticipated color, Adams Chapel School fulfills all other expectations and well represents the thousands of one-room school buildings which once dotted the nation's rural landscapes.

LOG CABIN AND POLE BARN

The country settled rapidly and houses were needed. At first there were no saw mills, and for sometime but few, so that sawed lumber could not be gotten at all, or only by long and expensive hauls. The consequence was that log houses were the rule.
    —George Brewer, "History of Coosa County," *Alabama Historical Quarterly*

One-room log cabin with loft; dovetailed joinery. Pole barn with rough-hewn planks; hand-sawed shingles

Using the material at hand, Alabama's early settlers built one- or two-pen log cabins as their first residences upon arrival. More affluent ones sent family members, sometimes with slaves, ahead to prepare housing for the family, but others quickly had to provide shelter as soon as they got to their new land. Some cabins were finer than others, but in each there were vital issues for a frontier family.

Was there a spring or well? Were there grazing lands for their animals? Were their fields productive? How far were the nearest neighbors? Would they ever see the friends and relatives they had left? What were the dangers, seen and unforeseen, that lurked beyond the clearing?

These thoughts plus so many others must have preyed on the minds of Alabama's pioneers. Even so, they came by the thousands, sometimes with wagon trains of possessions but more frequently with all their worldly goods in one wagon or oxcart. Many of these intrepid travelers even came on foot with just a knapsack of belongings. A hardy group, these settlers, in the grip of "Alabama Fever," were lured with promises of independence, land, cotton, and wealth. While many eventually built finer residences, most settlers lived in log cabins.

Skilled men constructed Old Alabama Town's log cabin in the prairie lands of south Montgomery County about 1820. Dovetailed corners, the most sophisticated means of joining logs, and the carefully scalped logs distinguished it from the cruder, rougher ones occupied by many pioneers. Oriented to the north-

Above: With a "morning porch" and an "afternoon porch," the log cabin offered comfortable work spaces for the pioneer housewife no matter the time of day. Opposite page: A simple structure, the pole barn provided shelter for the animals that played such important roles on the frontier.

west and southeast, the cabin's two porches provided shady places for morning and afternoon work.

Many years after the cabin's construction, someone covered it with clapboards, hiding the logs and giving it a completely different appearance. A later generation decided to tear down the old, worn, and dilapidated building, but when workman took off the outer layer, a handsome cabin emerged. Fortunately, the owners, Charles M. and Ellen Smith, realized what they had and immediately halted demolition. They restored the cabin as a guest house on their farm and then began a series of trips to the mountains of Tennessee and North Carolina to find appropriate furnishings. Most of the artifacts in the cabin today came from the Smiths' adventures in the coves and glens of the Smokey Mountains.

Following Mr. Smith's death, his widow donated the log cabin to Landmarks Foundation which moved it to Old Alabama Town as a 1976 Bicentennial project. It tells of social, economic, and cultural aspects of frontier life and the amazing survival abilities of those who lived it.

A simple construction of poles and vertical logs or planks, a pole barn was almost as important to settlers as their own cabins. In them they sheltered their animals, secured their tools, and harbored precious crops such as hay and corn. This replicated pole barn (the passageway to the log cabin) houses stalls, equipment, and an old log corncrib.

The farmer could drive his wagon into the barn and toss his corn over the top of the roofless crib. Corn was a basic need for man and beast. It provided meal and hominy for the family and feed for the animals. The lady of the house made shuck mops and stuffed mattresses, and little girls delighted in corn shuck dolls. Even the cobs were useful. Thus, a farmer with a full crib could rest a little easier at night knowing that it encased the answers to many needs.

THE WORKING BLOCK

Enter the Working Block through a gate set in a low stone wall banked with hedges. A wide dogtrot porch beckons you into the weathered Rose-Morris House, a superb example of a rural I-house. There a guide awaits you with a warm welcome and introduces you to the architectural and technological exhibits that so graphically depict some of the tools and the places of labor once prevalent in urban and rural areas.

In the country, cotton gins, grist mills, and blacksmith shops were sometimes conveniently located in proximity to each other, often at crossroads, providing services to farmers for miles around. With the cotton gin, work was seasonal as it was to some extent with the grist mill. The blacksmith, however, could ply his trade on a daily basis.

Farmers and their families often lived isolated lives, thus trips to the gin with a wagon load of cotton or to the mill with sacks of grain were exciting excursions looked forward to for days and relived over and over after the return home. The blacksmith produced many items for farmers and housewives and even made toys and metal puzzles for the children, so a visit to his shop was often a treat as well.

Of course, small towns also had these places of production, and in addition, there was a printer who put out the weekly newspaper and handled other printing jobs. A drugstore was often close by as well. Imagine the anticipation associated with a visit to the soda fountain: ice cream, sodas, and sundaes danced through young and old heads alike.

There were experts who kept engines running and presses rolling, but there were also individual craftspeople who performed one-person tasks with talent and skill and others who brought beauty and joy into often lonely lives—musicians, artists, and storytellers. You may encounter craftspeople or musicians during your visit. These people love to talk about what they do and may even let

A banjo player greets visitors in the Rose House dogtrot as they arrive for tours of the Working Block.

you share in the production—playing a musical instrument, painting a picture, or throwing the shuttle on the loom.

As you move through the block notice the cotton patch where you may pick during season, the fig and peach trees, a garden—these, too, are producing. At the gin, there is a handsome old farm bell that rang out the cycle of the day's work, and in times of trouble the alarm brought men from the fields and women from their labors to aid in whatever the emergency might be.

ROSE-MORRIS HOUSE

451 COLUMBUS STREET

West of this, on both sides of the Turnpike, there were a number of settlers, among them Green Holifield [who] built a good house on the road . . . and opened a good farm.
— George Brewer, "History of Coosa County," *Alabama Historical Quarterly*

Two-story frame I-house with one story pedimented portico

A significant example of nineteenth-century Alabama vernacular architecture, the Rose-Morris House is an I-house (sometimes referred to as Georgia Plain or Plantation Plain) with an open dogtrot. A two-story structure, it consists of an open dogtrot with one room over one room on each side. A one-story lean-to expands the living space, and the one-story pedimented portico adds a classical touch to the facade. The I-house was a prevalent style throughout the South with variations in porches and shed rooms. This

house is of particular importance as it is one of only a few remaining in the state.

An enclosed reverse-run stairway protected by a paneled door breaks the sweep of the wide dogtrot which nevertheless permits strong breezes to flow through. The wide board walls throughout the house have dates of birthdays, weddings, and anniversaries inscribed on them in pencil—virtual historical accounts of former occupants. Decorative touches include marbleized and granitized

Federal mantels surrounding the small fireplaces in each room and handsome cornice molding in the dogtrot hall.

The house originally stood about twelve miles north of Wetumpka, Alabama, on Highway 231 (the old Turnpike Road) on land purchased from the U.S. government in 1841 by Howell Rose, the first private owner of the property after the removal of the Creek Indians and the establishment of Coosa County. A native of Georgia, Rose had come to Alabama around 1818 and was a member of the Constitutional Convention of 1819. He owned the land until Green Holifield bought it in 1856. Elderly author George Brewer wrote his memoirs of Coosa County about 1917 and in it commented that Holifield built the house. While this may be the case, the Federal elements in it strongly suggest an earlier construction date.

A number of families subsequently owned the property, but in 1907 S. J. Morris bought it and 120 acres for $720 and farmed there for the rest of his life.

Opposite page: The Morris family purchased this house in the early twentieth century, and it remained in their hands until Landmarks Foundation acquired it in the 1980s. This image depicts two members of the Morris family, perhaps on their way to town. (Photo courtesy Landmarks Foundation) Above: The handsomely restored Rose-Morris House is the entrance to Old Alabama Town's Working Block.

A letter from a daughter-in-law noted, "Mr. and Mrs. James Samuel Morris had nine children—all born in this old house. One child . . . died the same day she was born. They raised eight children here and all worked on the farm." Mr. Morris died in 1952 and his wife in 1977 at the age of ninety-five.

In 1987, Landmarks Foundation acquired the house from a family member and faced a real challenge in moving it nearly thirty miles to Old Alabama Town. After studying every route and finding all unsatisfactory for one reason or another, the house mover, I. E. Davis, suggested cutting the house between floors,

The I-house with lean-to configuration. The brick used for the rebuilt chimneys is similar to that of the original.

bracing it carefully, placing the dollies under the first level, and then lifting the top floor with a crane. While this element was hanging in space, drivers would pull out the first floor on its dollies and then lower the second story onto a separate truck for the trip to town. Suspenseful and risky though it was, it worked, and the two pieces rode into Montgomery, one behind the other. Crews placed the first floor in the proper location, and the next day, the crane once again picked up the second and put it gently and exactly where it belonged atop its companion. Landscaping in the yard at the completion of restoration included privet hedges from the original site as well as some of the stone in the wall.

The restored house is the entrance to the Working Block where guides welcome guests for tours. Musicians gather regularly for the "Second Saturday Jam Session," and some type of musical demonstration is almost always available on the dogtrot or in the rooms of this handsome old house.

CLANTON KITCHEN

In spinning, a woman had to stand or walk back and forth as the rolls were drawn into thread and twisted by the turning of the wheel. . . . Not everyone owned a loom for it was a large mechanism for a log cabin. Enough were owned in a neighborhood to weave cloth for all, however.
—Everett Dick, *The Dixie Frontier*

Frame saddlebag structure with front porch

Although there was manufactured cloth available, many nineteenth-century women did spin and weave, producing textiles to clothe their families. Slave women were often in charge of the weaving room on large plantations, producing fabric for blacks' and whites' clothing. The Clanton kitchen, a two-room saddlebag structure, now houses looms, wheels, weasels, and sometimes spinners and weavers who demonstrate their venerable arts.

The building bears the name of General James Holt Clanton, a local Civil War hero who served in the conflict, resuming his law practice at its conclusion. In 1871, while trying a railroad case for the State of Alabama in Knoxville, Tennessee, he received a fatal wound on the street delivered by a man with whom he had argued in court. The people of Alabama, in honor and memory of his services, raised money to build a home for his widow and children on South Hull Street in 1872.

Long known as the "Clanton Cottage," the small Italianate house had a separate two-room kitchen and dining room, connected by a covered walkway. When Landmarks Foundation arranged for the Cottage Hill Foundation to move the endangered Clanton House to a new location, the Foundation brought the kitchen to Old Alabama Town for preservation.

Restored with a porch across the front, the Clanton kitchen and its spinning and weaving exhibits continue the story of nineteenth-century Alabama.

BLACKSMITH SHOP

The blacksmith was one of the most necessary persons in the community of early days.
—Mary E. Brantley, *From Cabins to Mansions*

Simple unpainted frame structure with overhang roof, wide doors; stone and brick forge

C elebrated in poetry and song, the village blacksmith was an integral part of society well into the twentieth century. While larger farms and plantations had their own resident "smithys," smaller operations and individuals depended upon the independent black smith for a variety of needs. Included in these necessities were horse and mule shoes, metal barrel hoops, rims for wagon wheels, and repairs to tools, utensils, and other equipment.

At Elmore County's Fleahop Crossroads in 1893, Daniel Webster Boatwright opened his blacksmith shop with accommodations in it for his brother to ply his carpentry trade. The Boatwright family operated the shop until the 1940s. The county then used it as a repair shop for road machinery for several

years. When the Boatwright heirs, Jim Boatwright and Grace Ford, sold the property in the 1980s, the shop was no longer in operation, and the family donated tools and furnishings to Landmarks Foundation. In 1994, new owners, Mr. and Mrs. Jesse Adams, gave the building to the Foundation for restoration in Old Alabama Town. A young college student, Dan Lavender, took on the project, assisting in moving the structure to Old Alabama Town and its restoration.

Much of the equipment on display is original to the shop, and the stone in the forge is native to Elmore County. A working blacksmith is frequently on duty demonstrating and discussing the techniques of this time-honored art.

Above: Working blacksmith demonstrates an ironworker's art. Opposite page: Daniel Boatwright, family, and employees display some of their handiwork in this turn-of-the-century photograph of the Boatwright Blacksmith Shop. (Photo courtesy Landmarks Foundation)

HAIGLER PLANTATION OFFICE

For business reasons, if no other, planters kept detailed and extensive records.
—Lucille Griffith, *Alabama: A Documentary History to 1900*

One-room frame building with replicated Greek Revival portico

A variety of outbuildings were essential to the operations of a nineteenth-century plantation, and an office for the owner and manager was often one of them. A one-room structure, the Haigler Plantation Office later became the kitchen when the original one burned. Pulled up and attached to the rear of the main house, the office had to give up its porch. Architect Nick Holmes designed the present pedimented and columned portico, creating a handsome, historically correct facade. The restored building is now a woodcrafter's shop.

Above: Originally the Graves-Haigler Plantation Office, this classic building served as the family kitchen after the first one burned. Opposite page: The restored office now houses a woodcrafter's shop. Below: This outbuilding was the Cram-Lakin kitchen and cook's quarters and now serves visitors to the Working Block.

CRAM-LAKIN OUTBUILDING

Located to the rear of the Cram-Lakin House stands a "saddlebag" whose original two rooms contained the kitchen and cook's quarters. Renovated, it now serves as curatorial storage and as public restrooms for the Working Block.

DRUGSTORE MUSEUM

On Saturdays, the customers crowded to the fountain, three deep, working the soda jerks to a frazzle. In Montgomery, the entire front of McGehee Brothers on Dexter Avenue was open. Customers would sit and sip 10 cent milkshakes in French cafe style, both observers and participants in the passing scene.

—Alabama Pharmaceutical Association, *Profiles of Alabama Pharmacy*

Double doors and display window

S ealed upon most minds is the image of the local drugstore with friendly druggist and soda jerk, an idea derived from reality, the movies, legend, and lore. In small towns, especially, the social life of young and old often revolved around the soda fountain, and from the pharmacy came healing and often foul tasting pills and liquids. Realizing that this cultural heritage was disappearing from late-twentieth-century America, the Alabama Pharmaceutical Association collected artifacts and established the drugstore museum in the early 1980s at another location.

In 1990 Landmarks Foundation and the APA together undertook moving the museum to Old Alabama Town where the Foundation replicated an interior setting in an on-site warehouse. Complete with soda fountain, patent medicines, a pharmacy, cosmetics, and appropriate tables and chairs, the drugstore museum depicts the scene as many remember it. A "model druggist" welcomes visitors and discusses on tape what his role had been in "yesterday's" drugstore.

Sadly, the soda fountain does not provide soda, ice cream, or shakes, but then neither does the pharmacy dispense its unpleasant but essential wares.

Above and below: Reminiscent of an earlier day, the drugstore museum brings back memories of chocolate sodas, fountain drinks, and medical concoctions, whose taste seemed to linger longer than their beneficial healing powers.

PRINT SHOP

Drink simply to the freedom of the press: though one would think it was sufficiently a free thing already. Considering how many take the papers without paying for them.
    —Johnson Jones Hooper, *Early Alabama Publications*

The hero of the story of publishing in frontier Alabama was the newspaper editor-printer. . . . He, perhaps even more than the itinerant schoolmaster, was the enlightener of the backwoods.
    —Rhoda Ellison, *Early Alabama Publications*

Storefront with windows in adapted masonry warehouse

D r. Rhoda Ellison's outstanding study of the earliest Alabama printers and publications notes 1807 as the year a paper first appeared in Wakefield, a small frontier community in what would become Alabama.

Between that time and the inauguration of Montgomery's first paper, the *Montgomery Republican*, which began publication in January 1821, printing circles had made great strides, stretching from one state boundary to the other. With some slight interruption in the 1820s and for a very few months after the Civil War, the city has had the services of a newspaper, and sometimes several simultaneously. A current publication, the *Montgomery Advertiser*, dates back to 1828 when the *Planters' Gazette* first appeared; the publisher changed the name in 1834 to the *Advertiser*, and it has been in continuous operation except at the end of the Civil War.

Old Alabama Town's print shop, appropriately located next door to the Drugstore Museum, reflects late-nineteenth- and early-twentieth-century techniques with equipment donated by the *Greenville Advocate*, the *Butler County News*, and a local Montgomery print shop. Included in the display are a Mergenthaler linotype, Babcock newspaper press, Kelsey hand press, C&P press, a Pearl letter press, a composing stone and other necessary tools for putting a newspaper to bed, getting it out on the streets, and taking care of a variety of printing orders.

Top left: In most urban areas small print shops produced the weekly paper that kept the citizenry informed. Another essential function of the shop was the printing of small jobs, such as advertisements and wedding and funeral notices. Top right and above: Equipment from the Greenville Advocate, *the* Butler County News, *and other shops enable Old Alabama Town to interpret the printing business in the days before computers.*

MOLTON OUTBUILDINGS

The saddlebag type was produced if the second pen was placed against the chimney end.
—Eugene Wilson, *Alabama Folk Houses*

Two frame saddlebag structures; entrances depict two different styles

T he Molton Outbuildings flanked the rear of the Molton House on the original site at the southeast corner of Adams Avenue and Union Street. Saddlebags, each structure had two front doors and a common chimney. They probably served as a kitchen and housing for servants, but later when domestic activities moved indoors, the two buildings provided homes for ladies living under the auspices of the Working Women's Association.

Landmarks Foundation moved the buildings in 1993. In one, the Foundation removed the center wall, providing space for an exhibit and meeting area where photographs depict "The Home Front, Montgomery's Domestic Architec-

These small saddlebag buildings flanked the rear of the Molton House on its original site at Union Street and Adams Avenue. The cantilevered overhang is typical of other structures of this kind in both urban and rural Alabama.

ture, 1820–1920." The other structure retains its center wall and houses basket and quilt displays. The exteriors received slightly different porch and step configurations both of which were typical in nineteenth-century Alabama.

COTTON GIN

The grand occupation of autumn is cotton picking. . . . The fine dark-green foliage is relieved by bunches of downy cotton of the purest white.
—Philip Gosse, *Letters from Alabama*

Everyone who raises cotton must have a gin.
—Anne Royalle, *Letters from Alabama, 1817–1822*

Replicated board and batten gin house with loading platform, shed along west side with scales

O ne of Landmarks Foundation's most impressive feats was the reassembly and restoration of a unique turn-of-the-century Continental cotton gin. Housed in a replicated "gin house," the intricate machinery interprets several dimensions of Alabama history and culture—social, agricultural, and technological.

Eli Whitney's patenting of the cotton gin in 1793 and 1794 opened the door for the growing of the short-staple, or green seed, cotton in the southern interior where environmental conditions blended almost perfectly for its cultivation. Until a practical "engine" for separating lint and seed appeared, it had not been economically feasible to plant and harvest such a crop. Whitney's gin paved the way for the development and manufacture of increasingly larger and more efficient machines.

According to early Alabama historian Albert J. Pickett, the first gin in Alabama was that of a Jewish veteran of the Revolution, Abram Mordecai, who came to the region in the 1780s as a trader. About 1802, he set up his gin, manufactured by Lyons and Barnett of Georgia which brought the equipment by pack horse and installed it near the future site of Montgomery. Unfortunately, because of continuing quarrels, the Indians burned the gin, stole Mordecai's livestock, and cut off his ear.

Other gins soon became available with Benjamin Hawkins, agent to the Creek Indians, who encouraged the growing, spinning, and weaving of cotton. Hawkins believed that in developing agricultural pursuits and domestic industries Native Americans would settle down to farming and a less-nomadic life. By the time of the Creek-American War of 1813–14, there were many engaged in such activities with cotton as one of the leading crops.

After the land cessions following the war, it was cotton that lured the settlers into Alabama with the price reaching the highest of the antebellum period in 1817. Travelers such as Anne Royalle often commented on the fields stretching into the distance and of the slaves who were tending them. Gin makers made the trek into the frontier, recognizing the needs of planters and the opportunities for themselves. One of these was a New Hampshire native, a carpenter and a house designer and builder, Daniel Pratt.

Pratt first came South in 1819, settling in Savannah, Georgia, for two years before moving to Milledgeville, Georgia, where he constructed several outstanding houses. In nearby Clinton, he joined Samuel Griswold, a gin manufacturer, and within a year was in charge of the operations. As Alabama's cotton production increased it lured Pratt further west, and in 1833 he loaded the materials for fifty gins and, with his wife and two slaves, made the trip over the Federal Road from Milledgeville to central Alabama.

Settling near Wetumpka, he built the gins and put them on the market. The next year, he rented lands near the Alabama River on Autauga Creek and when that lease expired, he purchased land further up the creek, founding the village of Prattville and building an industry that was to become international in scope.

As Alabama's first industrialist, Pratt advocated manufacturing as a means of making the South less dependent on the North. By the time of the Civil War, he had accrued a fortune and a reputation for excellence. Following the conflict, he continued to promote industrial progress and was instrumental in the development of mineral resources in the Birmingham area. After his death in 1878, his nephew, Merrill Pratt, and great-nephew, Daniel Pratt II, assumed direction of the Daniel Pratt Gin Company.

Toward the close of the nineteenth century, mergers of a number of gin manufacturers, including the Pratts, resulted in the formation of the Continental Gin Company. This organization, the world's largest producer of gins, still manufactures them in the nearby town of Prattville. Some of the buildings on the banks of Autauga Creek date from Pratt's time. At the turn of the century, Continental made the equipment that became the Old Alabama Town gin.

Originally erected at Teasley's Mill in southeast Montgomery County about 1900, this "plantation gin," operated first by Chappell Gray Sr. and later by his son, consists of two gin-stands composed of eighty saws that pulled the lint from

Cotton gins of this type were prevalent throughout Alabama's farming communities, most of them built by Continental Gin Company of Prattville, Alabama.

the seed. Other components carried out essential functions as the cotton progressed from individual bolls to bale. Another vital aspect of the process was the saving of the seeds that were necessary for the next planting as well as for fertilizer, cattle feed, and a variety of other uses.

When operating at full capacity, the gin averaged two bales an hour. Owners ginned their own crop and that of nearby farmers who brought the cotton in mule-drawn wagons. After ginning, 1,500 pounds of the staple produced a 500-pound bale and 1,000 pounds of seed. The cotton picking season at that period extended from mid-August to mid-November and during the peak times, this gin's five-man crew sometimes worked through the night. (Now the season can extend until Christmas because of new strains of cotton.)

This gin shut down in 1942, perhaps because of World War II and lack of help, but several factors contributed to the closing of small, two-stand gins of this type: larger, more commercial operations could handle the job more efficiently and, too, there was a steady postwar decline in the cultivation of cotton.

In the early 1980s, the owner planned to demolish the decaying old gin house and dispose of all machinery and parts. The fact that this gin had never been modernized made it totally unique with tremendous historic value. Recognizing these qualities, two longtime cotton farmers and gin operators, Tommy Oliver and Billy McLemore, offered to handle the dismantling of all the old equipment and to store it until Landmarks Foundation could carry out the restoration in Old Alabama Town.

By the late 1980s, the Foundation had acquired the land and was ready to begin the job. Several truckloads of large and small, greasy, broken bits of metal, battered wooden elements, various and sundry pieces of belting arrived on the future site of the gin. These elicited considerable comment and some dismay as to just how this pile of "junk" could ever be a cotton gin. There were, however, years of experience and wisdom prepared to handle the project.

Tommy Oliver supervised the undertaking with incredible skill and understanding, working closely with architect John Shaffer on the replication of the gin house and with the Landmarks Restoration Committee including its chair, Jim Loeb, and members Clay Dean and Fred Wilkerson. Essential to the success of the job was Landmarks Foundation's crew, under the supervision of foreman Charlie Burell. Funding for the endeavor came from individuals and businesses involved with cotton production and associated industries.

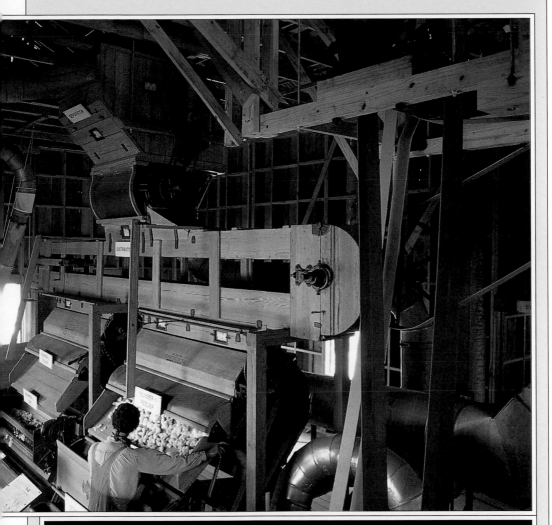

An operator watches as cotton tumbles into the gin for removal of seeds.

Completed in time for the bicentennial of the Whitney gin, the Old Alabama Town cotton gin officially opened in November 1993 with appropriate fanfare. Open six days a week with experienced guides, the cotton gin furnishes insight into many aspects of southern life and continues to explain the importance of cotton in its history and culture.

For further reading on cotton culture and ginning, see *A Narrative History of Cotton in Alabama and A Tour of the Old Alabama Town Cotton Gin*, by Dr. Thomas Oliver, available in the Old Alabama Town museum store.

GRIST MILL

I'll never forget how the warm cornmeal smelled as it came out of the hopper after having been crushed between the heavy millstones. It smelled so good that I could never resist the temptation to pick up a handful and eat it right fresh out of the mill. And it tasted almost as good as it smelled.
—Jese Culp, *The Good Ole Days*

Frame building with interior platform necessary to adequately elevate equipment

J ust as cotton was the staple and the money producer for many farmers, corn was the basic food crop. It was what fed the family and, of course, the farm animals upon which they all depended. Corn, ground into meal and grits, was the indispensable food upon which all families survived.

Rotating millstones, powered by some external force, were necessary to change corn from kernel to grist. In earlier times water or animals supplied the power. Steam, then electrical, kerosene, diesel, and gasoline engines provided the energy to produce peck after peck of meal, grits, and ground wheat for flour. The Old Alabama Town grist mill represents the many mills which helped feed Alabamians.

James Canary Green opened his grist mill in rural Randolph County early in the twentieth century and operated it until the time of his death in the early 1940s. Then his son, Herman Green, took over and ran it until the 1950s. A modern mill for its day, the equipment included a kerosene engine to power the heavy stones that ground the corn into the desired consistency.

Using as a model the long-used equipment given to it by the Green family in 1995, Landmarks replicated housing for corn-grinding elements.

Opposite page: This grist mill, dating from the turn of the century, ground thousands of bushels of corn for the neighbors of owner-operator James Canary Green in rural Randolph County until the 1960s. Above: Powered by man, water, animal, steam, kerosene, gasoline, diesel, or electricity, the grinding of grain has been an essential component in human existence.

ALONG THE STREETS OF OLD ALABAMA TOWN

Buildings from the nineteenth century lining North Hull Street create an ambience far different from the atmosphere of commercial and residential streets of today. Several houses are on their original sites, and over the past thirty years, Landmarks Foundation has moved others in to join them.

In the 1850s, North Hull Street was developing within the center of an upscale residential neighborhood. This characteristic was evident until the 1930s and 1940s when creeping decay and commercialism began taking their toll. Used car lots replaced cottages, and once proud houses gave way to bait shops and second-rate night spots. A few enduring souls clung to the remnants of this once quiet, neighborly place.

Landmarks Foundation began its restoration and development in 1967 and 1968 with its mission being not only to preserve Alabama's architectural and historic heritage but also to bring a blighted area back into a productive life. The Foundation has succeeded. The buildings serve multiple purposes, producing income and serving as museums. Together, they create a streetscape from the past.

Slowly walk along, imagining yourself on the front porch of a gingerbread cottage with cooking smells from your neighbors' suppers filling the air. Listen to the children playing hide-and-go-seek and chasing "lightning bugs" in the twilight.

Opposite page: A shady stroll along the streets of Old Alabama Town brings visitors face-to-face with the architecture of the nineteenth century. The Davis-Cook House displays transitional ideas, combining Italianate brackets, ventilator covers, and fanciful balustrade with a Greek Revival colonnade.

NORTH HULL STREET, EAST SIDE

WARE-FARLEY-HOOD HOUSE

440 NORTH HULL STREET

In the mid–nineteenth century, Montgomery was graced by one of the most outstanding assemblages of Italianate architecture in the South.
—Robert Gamble, Senior Architectural Historian, Alabama Historical Commission

Two-story frame structure with fretwork trimmed porches; cupola

As the Italianate style drifted southward, Montgomerians reacted with enthusiasm to the ideas and details embodied within it. Cupolas and fretwork tantalized builders, and during the 1850s these adornments added great variety and interest to the streetscape. The Ware-Farley-Hood House, sporting these elements, captures some of this fanciful ebullience while also demonstrating changes in attitudes toward health and comfort as well as advances in technology.

During the nineteenth century, ventilation and the circulation of "good air" became issues of great concern for scientists and lay people who fixed the blame for many epidemics on airborne miasmas. Good air could assure a healthier, more comfortable existence, and in the South, especially, builders searched for ways to defeat the heat. High ceilings were one means of reducing the amount of hot air at floor level, and cupolas with open windows provided this "bad" air with an escape route. Steam-powered machinery and the jigsaw produced elements such as small, decorative covers for attic ventilation, fretwork, and brackets, each of which reflect the mid-Victorians' combined interests in health and aesthetics.

In 1850, planter James A. Ware purchased half of a block on South Hull Street between Adams Avenue and Alabama Street as the residential town moved southward. Five years later, he sold the property for a considerably higher sum than he had paid, indicating that he had improved the property with the con-

The restored house indicates the abilities of architect, committee, and crew in determining the exterior details and elements.

struction of a dwelling. Banker James A. Farley was the next owner-occupant, and his family continued to live there until 1905 when the house became Starke's School for Girls. In 1908 the school closed, and the next year Horace Hood, newspaperman, one-time state legislator, and sheriff of Montgomery County, became the owner.

By this time, the neoclassical revival had brought columns back into fashion. Fretwork was no longer in vogue, and a number of Montgomerians were remodeling their homes, removing the outdated elements and replacing them with columns. Mrs. Susan Hood obviously wanted to be in style and also must have expressed a desire to move the house to another part of their property closer to the corner of Adams and Hull. Perhaps one of her reasons for moving the house 150 feet to the corner was that a mobile, growing population wanted to be away from the city center and property values were rising as people moved southward. The Hoods' property covered almost a quarter of the block, and by moving the house there was room for one other dwelling facing South Hull Street. The back of the lot on Decatur Street also allowed space for more development.

Abstracts tell fascinating stories, and that of this property reveals an interesting bit of information. Horace, knowing of Susan's wishes to move the house, gave her permission to do so with the stipulation that it had to be done within a two-month period. With mules, and many hands, the deed was accomplished.

After the move she renovated the dwelling, removing the porch and adding stylish columns and a dormer. At her death in 1936, her daughters inherited the property, and the two ladies lived there for many years. In 1956, after the death of one, the remaining sister sold the property to an insurance company that occupied the building until its late 1980s acquisition by Retirement Systems of Alabama (RSA) which needed land for a parking deck.

Just prior to RSA's donating the house and funds to assist in bringing it to Old Alabama Town, the Foundation had acquired a large lot, perfect for the Ware-Farley-Hood House. Moving any building is a challenge but a big two-story one presents multiple problems. Representatives from all parties involved met time and again, carefully assessing every possible route, noting tree limbs, power lines, and traffic patterns. Demolition crews began removing the columns and a back wing which would later be replaced. (The cupola had long since decayed and been demolished.) There was a feeling of great urgency since the construction crew of the parking deck indicated they would begin work on their schedule whether the house was still there or not. In other words, it had to be off the lot or else.

It seemed that all was in readiness when the day before the scheduled date a phone call from the mayor's office delivered disturbing news: the move would necessitate lowering an essential 911 line, and there was too much danger of interrupting vital services. The relocation could not take place as planned. Pleas for dispensation failed; the Foundation would have to wait until the city could run an alternate line. But the bulldozer engines of the parking deck crew were warming up on the site. In desperation, Landmarks Foundation personnel pointed out that there was a vacant lot within two blocks of Old Alabama Town and after frantic phone calls well into Friday night they received permission to park the house there temporarily.

This early photograph was the only guide that architect John Shaffer and the building committee of Landmarks Foundation had to guide the exterior restoration of the Ware-Farley-Hood House. (Photo courtesy Landmarks Foundation)

Early on a chilly late-October Saturday in 1989, the sturdy old structure began to slowly leave its foundation, the second time it had experienced this wrenching ordeal in its 139 years. Getting onto the street and traveling the first block presented no obstacles but in the next one, the house became pinned against a tree trunk, delaying progress for several minutes. Moving once again, it proceeded gracefully in front of the State Capitol as a reenactors' Confederate parade, with horses and cannon, advanced up Dexter Avenue.

Two other smaller structures that Landmarks Foundation and the Cottage Hill Foundation were rescuing for restoration were on the move that day, with the Ware-Farley-Hood House in the lead. It was a veritable parade of homes, and as the reenactors' cannons boomed and horses whinnied, someone remarked, "Once again we are evacuating Atlanta, but this time we are taking our houses with us."

All the while, crews were lowering and then rehanging various types of lines and cables as police motorcycles wheeled back and forth, directing traffic and keeping the throngs of onlookers at bay.

By early afternoon, the big house was on its temporary lot and all involved breathed sighs of relief. Landmarks Foundation officials felt a kinship with Susan Hood, who had received a two-month ultimatum from her husband. Landmarks had also received a warning; the house movers stated they would leave their steel beams under the structure for only two months without extra charge. At the end of that period, however, they would have to bill another ten thousand dollars.

The city was putting in another 911 line down Jefferson, a street the house had already crossed, and Landmarks Foundation watched the work with bated breath, hoping the crews would finish within the deadline, before further expenses came into the picture. By early December the line was in place.

It was a very cold Saturday when the next move got under way from the lot that happened to be next door to a somewhat derelict all-night bar. As the huge load teetered onto the street, the customers of the establishment, bleary-eyed and unbelieving, vowed to sober up and never touch another drop. By noon the house was on its fourth and final resting place, ready for restoration to its original, Italianate character. The only problem was that no one knew what that had been although efforts to solve the mystery were ongoing.

Finally, a telephone call came from an elderly lady, a historian in her own right and a cousin of the Farley family, who had found a catalog from Starke's School for Girls with a picture of the house on the cover. It was from this one picture and an old newspaper photograph of the cupola that architects and builders carried out the restoration of the Ware-Farley-Hood House. It once again looks as it did with fretwork adorned porches, a stunning replicated cupola, and a replaced back wing.

The interior, designed with a central hall, has a handsome front-run staircase broken by one landing. On the north side are magnificent double parlors which lead into a dining room extending across the rear. Access to the cupola is by stairs from the second floor that lead to an attic where a crooked flight goes on to the top.

This "house on wheels" has now found its permanent home. A significant part of Montgomery's past and of Old Alabama Town, its elegance attracts admiring glances from all who pass.

MAP 12   ALONG THE STREETS   83

CRAM-LAKIN HOUSE

420 NORTH HULL STREET

The Montgomery Theatre—A look into the new theatre last evening satisfied us that D. H. Cram, who has designed it entirely, deserves a great deal more credit than we supposed, for the elegant, recherche and commodious appointments of the establishment.
—Montgomery Daily Mail, 11 October 1860

Five-bay symmetrical frame cottage with Italianate bracketing and ventilator covers

L ocated on its original site, the Cram-Lakin Cottage (familiar name: Lakin House) dates from the mid-1850s. Daniel Cram, a civil engineer and superintendent of the Montgomery and West Point Railroad, built the house about the time of his 1857 marriage to the granddaughter of town founder John Scott. Recognized as the designer of the Montgomery Theatre, Cram may well have drawn the plans for both his own home and that of his neighbor, Thomas De Wolfe whose home originally stood a block east.

Almost identical to the De Wolfe-Cooper Cottage except for the porch, the house has four rooms arranged around a T-shaped center hall whose back area creates a fifth room. The bracketing and ventilator covers are the same on both houses as are the doors, windows, and surrounds.

Josephus Lakin came to Montgomery from St. Louis after the Civil War and established a photographic gallery on Market Street. Through the years, he gained distinction, winning awards and honors for his work. His great-grandson, Milo B. Howard, late state archivist and renowned preservationist, was one of the founders of Landmarks Foundation, and the house carries Lakin's name in Milo's memory.

Around the turn of the century, owners radically altered the house, changing the front porch and adding a pyramidal roof with a front dormer, a popular technique of the day. In the early 1960s, a new owner, Tom Neville, acquired

Still on its original site, this cottage, built by engineer Daniel Cram, was later the home of Josephus Lakin, a noted late-nineteenth-century photographer.

it as headquarters for his plumbing concern which he operated for more than twenty years.

Landmarks Foundation acquired the house that, thanks to Neville's occupancy and use, had survived when most surrounding structures suffered the dismal fate of urban decline and demolition. During restoration, the Foundation replaced the porch with an appropriate one for its period.

GRAVES-HAIGLER HOUSE

410 NORTH HULL STREET

I spent many happy hours in this house between 1930 and 1960.
  —Blanche Haigler (David Haigler's wife), 1986

I made my first quarter sweeping this hall.
  —Willie "Buster" Smith (son of Ella Smith, the family cook and a
  neighborhood midwife), 1983

Deep South adaptation of a story-and-a-half tidewater cottage; end chimneys, porch with rough-hewn square cypress columns and an el wing

owndes County, formed in 1830 from parts of Montgomery, Butler, and Dallas Counties, attracted settlers to its rich soil which pioneers soon determined was well suited to the growing of cotton. The Graves family of Georgia came in 1817, soon after the opening of central Alabama land sales, and in 1841, Y. W. Graves built this house. In 1846 he sold it to Josiah Haigler.

Haigler, a native of South Carolina, and his first wife had eight children, and after her death in 1852 he married her widowed sister, who had three children. In 1854 the couple had a son, Lewis. Although one of Josiah's children had died, there was still a large number of offspring for the parents to raise.

According to family stories, it was about this time that the Haiglers built the two-room el wing and moved into it, leaving the eleven children to occupy the two dormitory-like upstairs rooms. There was no door connecting these rooms; enclosed staircases, one on each side of the house, were the only access to the quarters occupied on one side by girls and on the other by the boys.

The main body of the Graves-Haigler House is a story-and-a-half Deep South adaptation of the more rigidly designed cottages of the Tidewater region. Prototypes of this particular house occur in eastern North Carolina, illustrating the changes made as builders adjusted structures to place and personal preferences.

Joined to it by an inset columned porch is a saddlebag el wing. The interior of the bigger house, built following the dogtrot plan, exhibits characteristics quite sophisticated for antebellum Lowndes County and portrays the care and concern given by householders to the mainstreams of fashion. Fine flame mahogany graining on the hall dado and doors reflect the touch of a master artist as do the marbleized mantles and the floor, checkerboarded and also marbleized, in what must have been the parlor.

A door in a back room led to the outside kitchen, but when it burned many years ago the family pulled up the plantation office, attaching it to the rear for a kitchen. A Federal mantle in this small building expresses further the builder's architectural awareness.

Members of the Haigler family continued to occupy the house until the early 1960s. General Electric purchased hundreds of acres in Lowndes County in the late 1970s for the construction of a plastic plant, and in order to get Environmental Protection Agency licenses, GE had to save certain historic buildings located on the property. Descendants of the Haigler family, Dr. and Mrs. David Irwin, owned the house and donated it to Landmarks Foundation at the time they sold to GE. In 1983, the Foundation

moved the structure to town with some financial assistance from the corporation. Separating the el wing and the former plantation office from the main building, the Davis House Movers lined them up, creating a veritable house parade on the over-twenty-mile trip into Montgomery.

Information from nineteenth-century census records revealed that one of the products of the Haigler Plantation was honey from their beehives, and when preparations began for the move, strenuous efforts were necessary to get descen-

Opposite page: This is the first view that Landmarks Foundation officials had of the sadly deteriorated Graves-Haigler House, a prominent house in rural Lowndes County in the 1840s. (Photo courtesy Landmarks Foundation) Above: Today the restored Graves-Haigler House reflects the vision and determination of Landmarks Foundation's board, staff, and restoration crews.

dants of those bees out of the walls of the house. The bee eradication proved incomplete, for as the movers took the three buildings out across the pastures, a long line of bees trailed behind; many became urbanites as they followed the houses all the way to town. Another passenger on that trip was a snake that had hidden itself away in the wing; however, this creature did not have the opportunity to become acclimated to a new environment, as a workman quickly dispatched it after discovery.

Paint analysis revealed the grained and marbleized areas, and although later occupants had painted over the graining, they had left the inside of a stairway door intact. From this, master grainer, Rock Headley, who also did the work in the Young, Thompson, Molton, and Martin-Barnes Houses, was able to re-create the beautiful faux work of the earlier artist.

DAVIS-COOK HOUSE AND COOKHOUSE

360 AND 220 NORTH HULL STREET

Formerly the capitol clock could be seen from the front porch of this house which is [was] situated on one of the city's highest hills.
 —*Official Guide to the City of Montgomery,* 1948

Porch across front with strong, boxed columns; cornice brackets and ventilator covers

Book dealer Ben Davis built his home in 1857 at the crest of the Bibb Street hill where it had a commanding view of downtown and the state capitol. The time was one of architectural transition, and the columned Greek Revival fashion was giving way to the bracketed, asymmetrical Italianate style. Some builders, however, incorporated elements of both in their designs. Such was the case with Davis who used a colonnaded porch across the front of his rigidly symmetrical house, but on the cornice he lavishly applied graceful brackets interspersed with decorative ventilator covers, thus embodying handsome details from two important architectural periods.

A dogtrot hall divides the house whose five high-ceilinged rooms assure some respite from the summer sun. Other cooling devices are the floor-length windows across the front porch. When open, they permit breezes to flow, pulled through the deep porch which offers protection from both sun and rain.

Moved in 1973 when the widening of its street became imperative as an access road to Interstate 65, the house seemed reluctant to leave the original site. As the moving crew took it off the lot and into the streets, it became stuck in the intersec-

Opposite page: The Davis-Cook House had a commanding view of downtown Montgomery from its original location. During the 1930s and 1940s, it was a tourist home and the residence of Mrs. Marie Cook. (Photo courtesy Landmarks Foundation) Above: Moved to Old Alabama Town, the Davis-Cook now graces the corner of North Hull and Columbus Streets.

tion, blocking traffic overnight and creating quite a stir among local businesses, especially a motel whose entrance was impassable. The next day, after considerable maneuvering, the building continued on to Old Alabama Town with no further problems. Restored, the Davis-Cook House (familiar name: Cook House) lends a gracious ambience to the corner of Columbus and North Hull Streets.

The original kitchen and cook's quarters, a two-room saddlebag structure, stood behind the big house. Landmarks Foundation acquired and moved both in 1973 at the same time. However, the lot was not big enough for the two, so the smaller building, affectionately known as the Cook House Cookhouse is behind the Campbell Cottage at 220 North Hull Street.

MAYOR REESE COTTAGE

340 NORTH HULL STREET

"Warren Reese Announces for Mayor"
  —*Montgomery Daily Advertiser*, 24 March 1885

"Warren Reese Elected Mayor"
  —*Montgomery Daily Advertiser*, 6 May 1885

Greek Revival Cottage with hipped roof and boxed columns

A lthough the cottage was not built by Warren Reese, he occupied it at the time he was serving his two terms as mayor of Montgomery, 1885–89. This was during the exhilarating and progressive 1880s when Montgomery was experiencing its second "urbanization." The mule-drawn streetcar came in 1885, followed by the electric trolley the next year. At the same time, the city initiated work on a superb water system and erected the magnificent baroque fountain in Court Square's Artesian Basin.

Dating from the mid-1850s, the Mayor Reese Cottage is a beautifully proportioned Greek Revival dwelling, typical of many which once dotted the landscape of central Alabama towns. A one-story clapboard cottage, it originally stood at the SW corner of Alabama and Decatur Streets, about four blocks south of the business district.

A low, hipped roof extends over a full-length inset front porch distinguished by six boxed columns. The interior, on the ubiquitous T-shaped central hall plan, has four rooms flanking the hall that widens at the rear, creating a fifth room. A common configuration, this area frequently served as the dining room. A back door would have led to the outside kitchen.

Descendants of Mayor Reese donated the house to Landmarks Foundation which moved it in the early 1970s to Old Alabama Town. Restored, it is an ideal office for small organizations or businesses.

The Historic American Building Survey of the 1930s noted the Reese Cottage as the best example of a Greek Revival cottage in Montgomery. Note the difference between these square columns and the more delicate Federal ones on the Martin–Barnes House.

MARTIN-BARNES HOUSE

320 NORTH HULL STREET

Judge Abram Martin died at the home of his son-in-law, Dr. W. O.
Baldwin. . . . He was an able, honest and industrious lawyer.
  —Obituary, *Montgomery Advertiser and Mail*, 3 January 1875

He [Elly Ruff Barnes] and his father conducted the Barnes School for Boys
in Montgomery . . . and became principal of the school after his
father's retirement.
  —Thomas M. Owen, *History of Alabama and Dictionary of*
    Alabama Biography

Deep South adaptation of tidewater cottage with pedimented Federal portico and slender, chamfered columns

O ne of the oldest remaining houses in Montgomery, the Martin-Barnes House demonstrates the architectural transitions that took place as goods and materials became plentiful. Simple vernacular log or rough-hewn frame houses were giving way to more comfortable, stylish dwellings. This house, based on the dogtrot plan with rooms opening off a central hall, reflects the influence of the Federal style in the reeding on door and window surrounds. A reverse-run stair leads to the upper half-story.

An early settler in Montgomery, lawyer Abram Martin, built his home at the crest of the South Court Street hill about 1834. A few years after Martin's death in 1875, the family sold the house, which, according to an appraiser, was "old and of an old style." A new owner moved it around the corner onto Wilson Street and modernized it, adding gables with windows on the front, extending the porch and adorning it with Eastlake trim. It looked this way when schoolmaster Elly Barnes acquired the house in the early twentieth century.

In 1981, Landmarks removed the additions to the house, brought the house to Old Alabama Town, and restored it to the earlier period with a replicated Federal front portico designed by restoration architect Nicholas Holmes.

Barnes conducted the highly respected Barnes School for Boys for many years on Clayton Street in an 1830s house now known as the Figh-Pickett House. The Montgomery County Historical Society has relocated this house from its original Clayton Street site and restored it on South Court Street.

Reflecting architectural influences from the Tidewater region of Virginia and the Carolinas, the Martin-Barnes House is one of the oldest structures in Montgomery, dating from the 1830s.

CAMPBELL-HOLTZCLAW COTTAGE

220 NORTH HULL STREET

Gold and silver watches, diamonds in rings and pins for ladies and gents, latest style jewelry, silverware, plated ware, sporting goods including guns, pistols, and fishing tackle.

> —Advertisement from John Campbell, jeweler, *Montgomery Advertiser*, 18 May 1854

He [James Holtzclaw] began the study of law in the offices of Elmore and Yancey in 1853.

> —Thomas M. Owen, *History of Alabama and Dictionary of Alabama Biography*

One-story frame cottage with Greek Revival portico defined by boxed columns

ne of the exciting benefits of history is that it often reveals secrets. Just when historians think they have it all figured out, another scrap of information will cause a complete reassessment. This is the case with the Campbell Cottage.

Located next door to the Ordeman House, this cottage was a part of Landmarks' original purchase. The abstract stated that Charles Ordeman sold the house to John Campbell in 1853. Earlier research had led to the conclusion that Ordeman, an architect, had built this house on the south portion of his property and sold it to Campbell, perhaps to help defray some of his mounting debts.

However, the discovery that Ordeman never lived in the house made it necessary to take another look at this cottage. The current theory is that the house was in existence when Ordeman bought the property in 1850 and that he and his wife, Sarah, lived there while building the house next door. The Ordemans left Montgomery in late summer 1853, and in July Campbell bought the house. Civil War general James Holtzclaw later occupied it.

Later owners modernized the clapboard cottage with a new roof and porch. When Landmarks Foundation began work in 1973, crews found the earlier roof, enabling a restoration of the old roofline. The porch was replaced with a replicated Greek Revival portico based on others in the region. In 1974 the restored cottage became the headquarters of Landmarks, housing the Joggling Board, an antique and candy shop. Upon the completion of Lucas Tavern, Landmarks moved its offices and the Reception Center to that location.

The interior layout follows the common pattern of two large front rooms with a short reception hall that widens in the rear with a room to each side of it. Landmarks leases the house to businesses.

A tidy cottage with green shutters and a picket fence typified the dreams of many Alabamians during the nineteenth century. Jeweler John Campbell purchased this house from architect Charles Ordeman in 1853 and lived there for several years.

THOMPSON MANSION

401 MADISON AVENUE

After the hand-shaking, the President and party will be driven to Mrs.
W. P. Thompson's residence where a reception will take place.
  —Program of President McKinley's Visit to Tuskegee, Alabama Friday,
    16 December 1898

Front: Modified Corinthian columns and capitals, second-floor
balcony with iron lyre balustrade; sides: arcaded lattice porches;
rear: octagonal columns

B uilt about 1850 in Tuskegee, Alabama, an antebellum market town and educational center, the Thompson House represents a high point in pre–Civil War cotton-generated wealth. There is some question as to whether a small structure built by settler Peter Coffee Harris later received massive additions and alterations by Judge Thomas S. Tate, who acquired the property in 1850. Some believe that Tate built this handsome structure from top to bottom. Whatever the case, it was his home until after the Civil War when it became a hotel for a brief time.

In 1880, William P. Thompson bought the house. Planter, merchant, banker, sheriff of Macon County, and mayor of Tuskegee at the time of his death in 1891, Thompson was the father of twelve sons and two daughters. One son, Joseph, was prominent in Alabama's Republican Party and for eleven years served as U.S. Collector of Internal Revenue for the Districts of Alabama and Mississippi during the administrations of Theodore Roosevelt and William Howard Taft. In 1898, the Thompsons lavishly entertained President William McKinley who was speaking at Tuskegee Institute.

Another Thompson son, Charles, was a staunch Democrat, serving in the Alabama Senate and the U.S. House of Representatives. He died while in office, and his funeral was at the family home in Tuskegee with many national figures in attendance.

Restored in Old Alabama Town, the Thompson Mansion still attracts admirers from far and near.

William's son, farmer and businessman Grover Cleveland Thompson, lived in the house until his death in 1950. His widow, Annie Lee, lived there until she went to a nursing home in the 1970s.

Dating from flush times, the Thompson House is a grand mixture of architectural modes and tastes. A symmetrical Greek Revival house, its front columns present an adapted interpretation of Corinthian capitals while those in the rear are octagonal, a design sometimes seen on other structures in the region. Cast iron lyres compose the balustrade of the upstairs balcony. In addition to these classical elements, the house sports brackets, ventilator covers, and arcaded side porches characteristic of the Italianate style that was beginning to make dramatic statements around Alabama.

The builder demonstrated great concern for the climate with transept halls which allowed cross breezes in the summer. In the winter, small rooms and un-

Superbly blending several architectural styles, the Thompson Mansion reflects the aesthetic and economic highs of the 1850s. Columns on the front and back, brackets, fanciful ventilator covers, and arched latticed side porches are features that have made passersby stop and look for over 150 years. In 1902 the family gathered for this photograph. When William McKinley visited Tuskegee in 1898, the Thompsons had a reception at their home in his honor. The arch, erected for the occasion, had roses entwined through it. (Photo courtesy Landmarks Foundation)

usually low ceilings permitted the fireplaces to adequately warm spaces. Elegant plaster cornices and pedimented interior doors in the halls and a cantilevered, curving staircase combined with several types of graining and marbleizing portrayed an awareness of the varied and changing fashions of the period.

For almost one hundred years, the house had been the centerpiece of the large Thompson family, but Miss Annie Lee was the last to live in Tuskegee. The Alabama Exchange Bank of Tuskegee purchased the property, adjacent to the downtown business district, with the intention of demolishing the structure to make way for a new bank building. In order to clear the lot, in 1982 they sold the house to Hayes Gilliam of Bowdoin, Georgia, who had admired it during his years at Auburn University. Gilliam carefully and meticulously dismantled the house, mark-

ing every piece, even the pegs, photo-
graphing the entire process, and detailing the framing. He loaded the elements
onto trucks and carried them back to
Georgia for storage until he could reas-
semble it as his own home.

Landmarks Foundation officials
had long searched for an appropriate
columned house, but when they heard
about the Thompson Mansion, Gilliam
was already under way with his project.
Even though it was in Georgia warehouses, the Foundation continued to
hope that perhaps it could someday
return to Alabama. Just before Christmas of 1987, the call came from
Gilliam asking if Landmarks Foundation would like to discuss a possible
purchase of the elements. The Foundation was, of course, interested and,
with a very generous grant from the

*Delicately arched lattices shade
porches on east and west sides of
Thompson Mansion.*

Montgomery Kiwanis Club, it acquired the many pieces of the old dwelling.

In January 1988, Landmarks Foundation dispatched large trucks, usually
employed to haul cotton bales, to bring the treasure back to Alabama and to
Montgomery: beams, studs, mantels, doors, windows, pegs, columns, brackets,
plaster moulds, and flooring. It took seven loads to get it all to Old Alabama
Town where it went into a warehouse for safe-keeping.

In September of that year, reconstruction began. Referring to it as "the world's
largest jigsaw puzzle," architects, board members, consultants, and crew pon-
dered the project from every angle. Because of the elevation of the land, it was
possible to place the structure on a basement, and with a brick floor and exposed
beams, that "created" a historically replicated area similar to other like spaces
in nineteenth-century Alabama houses. Once the crew completed the basement,
their job took on great excitement as the walls went up, the roof went on, columns rose, and the grand building reappeared. In May 1991, the Visitor Center
for the Montgomery Chamber of Commerce opened to the public in the Thomp-

Roses start their climb up Thompson Mansion's Gothic arbor.

son Mansion and remained at that location until its move to Union Station in early 1999.

During the 1930s, the Historic American Building Survey (HABS), sponsored by the National Park Service, the American Institute of Architects, and the Library of Congress, provided jobs for historians and architects, hard-hit by the Great Depression, to research, draw plans, and photograph significant buildings for inclusion in this monumental study of America's building past. The Thompson House received recognition as being worthy of recording for posterity; these records were invaluable in the reconstruction of this magnificent structure which proudly presides over the corner of Madison Avenue and North Hull Streets at the entrance to Old Alabama Town.

NORTH HULL STREET, WEST SIDE

"BALTIC AVENUE" GINGERBREAD COTTAGES

325, 321, 317, AND 313 NORTH HULL STREET

Everybody is in search of a house who has to rent; new homes are in demand [with] prices keeping up remarkably well, too.
—*Montgomery Advertiser*, 23 August 1895

Four frame cottages adorned with gingerbread

L ovingly known as "Baltic Avenue," the four small cottages on the west side of North Hull Street are original to their sites. Built as rental property in the 1890s, they were the homes of shopkeepers, teachers, railroad workers, and clerks. Three are identical with front gables and wrap-around porches adorned with gingerbread. The fourth, a bit larger, has a porch across the front and gables which also sport those wonderful spindles, spools, and other wooden elements jigsaws made possible.

Four 1890s gingerbread cottages, built as rental property and lovingly known as "Baltic Avenue," create their own distinctive ambience in Old Alabama Town. (As most know, the Monopoly game's Baltic Avenue was a low-price property close to some very expensive real estate.)

DEWOLFE-COOPER COTTAGE

309 NORTH HULL STREET

October, 1849: John McCormack sold out the "Advertiser" to Mr. P. H. Brittan. Shortly thereafter, Mr. Thomas D. Wolfe [sic] merged the "State Gazette" into the same paper and united with Mr. Brittan.
   —M. P. Blue, "A Brief History of Montgomery," 1878

Italianate cottage with Steamboat Gothic latticed porch; brackets and ornamental ventilator covers

I n 1969, with the Ordeman House restoration progressing, Landmarks Foundation moved its first house, the deWolfe-Cooper Cottage, which dates from the mid-1850s. Newspaper editor Thomas deWolfe built his home on the corner of Columbus and Bainbridge Streets.

   Along with his friend P. H. Brittan, deWolfe edited the *Advertiser and State Gazette*, one of the leading newspapers of central Alabama. The deWolfes lived

Although slowly falling apart, the 1850s DeWolfe-Cooper Cottage stood on Columbus Street, bravely retaining its gracefully arched lattice porch, brackets, and decorative ventilator covers while hoping for help. (Photo courtesy Landmarks Foundation)

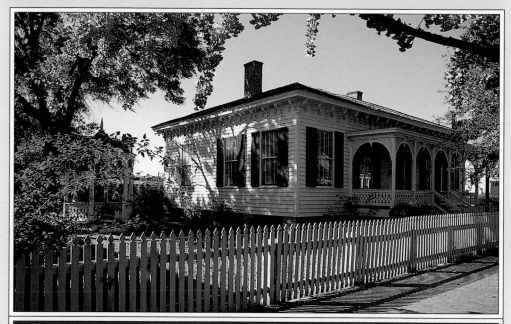

Help did arrive as the Landmarks Foundation brought the cottage to North Hull Street, the Foundation's first move. The restored DeWolfe-Cooper Cottage still boasts its handsome Italianate elements.

in a prosperous middle-class neighborhood near Brittan who occupied a brick house in the same block. Close by was railroad engineer Daniel Cram in a house almost identical in size and design to deWolfe's.

Italianate elements, such as brackets and fanciful ventilator covers, outline the cornice, but the inviting, arched latticed front porch is steamboat gothic, a popular style at the time. The house has the typical interior of the period with a T-shaped hall that widens into a much larger chamber to the rear. Two rooms open to each side of the central hallway. Between the front and back halls are double-paneled doors with glass lights.

Mrs. Annie Cooper was the house's last private resident, and it was from her that Landmarks Foundation acquired it in 1970. Moved about three blocks from its original site, the Cooper Cottage underwent restoration almost simultaneously with the Ordeman House. When the house museum opened in 1971, this lovely smaller cottage was ready to serve as a reception center and offices. Later, as other buildings took on those roles, it housed a number of civic groups and businesses.

BUSH COTTAGE

301 NORTH HULL STREET

Mr. J. F. Jackson is building a comfortable one-story residence on Union Street.
   —Montgomery Daily Mail, 19 July 1860

One story with inset porch with strong boxed column; appliqués in cornice

Built as rental property by lawyer Jefferson Franklin Jackson in 1860, the Bush Cottage is a "half-house" composed of a side hall with two adjoining rooms opening off it and a small room and porch behind. Homes of this type proliferated as Montgomery grew and prospered in its exhilarating role as state capital.

Although designed for tenants, the house reflects the period's love of adornment with square columns and fanciful balustrades beckoning one to sit on the porch. Originally at the corner of North Union and East Jefferson Streets, it had a companion house, also built by Jackson, located behind it on Union Street with similar detailing and styling.

Named for its last occupant, Mrs. Fannie Bush, the cottage made its 1982 Old Alabama Town entry after a rather exciting four-block trip down a major thoroughfare, Madison Avenue. During the ride, a bathroom addition fell off in the midst of noonday traffic, but since there was no damage except to this feature that had to be removed anyway, the Foundation philosophically shrugged and proceeded with the restoration. Since its completion, the handsome cottage has housed a number of local agencies and organizations.

NALL-YOUNG HOUSE

231 NORTH HULL STREET

Mary Harrison, who was married to Brooke William Young, inherited the Young Plantation from her aunt and uncle, Elizabeth Deane and J. P. Nall. Cotton was the chief crop and there was a cotton gin on the place.
—Beri Young Barfield, 1983

One story with columned portico, Greek Revival house attached by latticed porch to earlier cottage in rear

O riginally located in Burkville, a rural community in Lowndes County, the Nall-Young House is actually two structures that demonstrate an early, practical way to preserve the old with the new. A two-room and loft cottage was the first house constructed on the site by settler John Nall who came to Alabama from North Carolina. In 1820 he married Elizabeth Deane of Georgia, and in 1825 he purchased property in what was then a part of Montgomery County. (The legislature of Alabama formed Lowndes County in 1830 from parts of Montgomery, Dallas, and Butler Counties.) No novices to style, the Nalls included Federal mantles and dados topped by chair rails in their rural home.

In the 1850s, prospering from the growing of cotton, the planter built a finely detailed Greek Revival house on the dogtrot plan with four spacious,

An early-twentieth-century traveling photographer captures the images of three generations of the Young family, their servants, and pets in the front yard of their rural Lowndes County home. (Photo courtesy Landmarks Foundation)

A Greek Revival portico details the facade of the Nall-Young House.
The original cottage is visible to the left.

high-ceilinged rooms. Its features, too, reveal the Nalls' tastes for the fashions of the day. Greek "ears" boldly surmount interior door and window surrounds that, with the doors, sport handsome oak graining; marbleized mantles add other decorative touches. A thoughtful and practical man, Nall preserved his original cottage and united it with the larger structure by a latticed porch.

The Nalls had no children, but a niece, Mary E. Harrison, lived with them after the death of her parents. In 1851 she married Brooke Young, a native of Maryland who had come South. The Youngs lived with the Nalls and after the elder couples' deaths in the 1870s, Mary inherited the plantation; her husband and later her son continued the farming operations.

Descendants of the family owned the house until the 1980s when General Electric bought hundreds of acres to build a plant for the production of a specialized plastic. The company asked Landmarks Foundation to take the Nall-Young and Haigler Houses to Old Alabama Town for preservation and contributed funds to assist with the moves. The Nall-Young House arrived in Old Alabama Town in 1985.

JEFFERSON STREET

GALLAGHER HOUSE

422 EAST JEFFERSON STREET

As an evidence of the steady and continuous growth of Montgomery, over two thousand homes have been built here since 1880.
—*A Sketch of Montgomery, Alabama,* 1885

Late Italianate town house with bracketed cornice

Businessman James Gallagher built this house for his family in 1882. His widow left it to their daughter, Mary, a schoolteacher who lived there until her death in 1969.

Originally located at 114 North Hull Street, only a block from Old Alabama Town, the house represents a period of returning prosperity after the Civil War and Reconstruction. A two-story clapboard structure with paired cornice brackets, it retains Italianate characteristics that were once prevalent in this area.

Landmarks Foundation purchased the house in 1972 and sold it to an architect, Arthur Joe Grant, who restored and leased it for offices until 1999 when he decided to sell the property for commercial development, stipulating in the sale that the house was to be moved to Old Alabama Town. The new owners of the land, Maxwell Federal Credit Union, contributed to the cost of moving the house in November 1999. Restored, it will serve as rental space.

A comfortable, stylish 1880s residence, the Gallagher House displays Italianate detailing.

NOBLE HOUSE

434 EAST JEFFERSON STREET

The next revival was held in 1848. . . . The number of converts was not recorded. But at this time two significant additions were Cyrus Phillips and B. F. Noble . . . who were mainstays of the church during the next generation.
—Lee N. Allen, *The First 150 Years, First Baptist Church, Montgomery, Alabama*

Two-story brick house with hipped roof topped with metal cresting

B F. Noble, a banker and real estate investor, built his home on East Jefferson Street about 1850 as the area north of Madison Avenue began developing as a very upscale neighborhood. Both Noble and his wife were active in the affairs of Montgomery's First Baptist Church.

A two-story brick structure, their home underwent drastic modifications in the late 1940s as the neighborhood became more and more commercial. Ben Wilbanks, a tire and automobile dealer, saved the building and modified it with various additions to accommodate his needs, preserving the handsome interior staircase, several doors, and the "Greek eared" window and door surrounds.

Landmarks Foundation, long aware of the house, purchased it in 1998 and will carry out extensive research for its restoration. This includes the demolition of the attachments in order to conduct archaeological work to determine as much as possible about the site and the configuration of both the front and rear elevations. The Sanborn Fire Insurance maps, indispensable tools for preservation research, already have answered several questions including the location of several outbuildings that once stood on the site.

COLUMBUS STREET

BRITTAN-DENNIS HOUSE

507 COLUMBUS STREET

October, 1849: John McCormick sold out the "Advertiser" newspaper to Mr. P. H. Brittan.
    —M. P. Blue, "A Brief History of Montgomery"

Brick cottage with colonnaded porch; paired cornice brackets; etched ruby glass in sidelights and transom

B uilt in the 1850s by newspaperman Patrick Henry Brittan, this handsome house is the city's finest remaining brick cottage from the mid–nineteenth century. Brittan edited state and local papers including the *Montgomery Advertiser* and the *Daily Messenger*. In

The to-be-restored Brittan-Dennis House stands on its original site.

1859 the state legislature elected him secretary of state, a post he occupied throughout the Civil War.

Until 1957, the house was a residence, but from that year until the late 1980s it was the well-known antique and repair shop of Mr. and Mrs. J. W. Dennis. Landmarks Foundation acquired the property in 1994 and plans an eventual restoration.

Built as fashion changed from Greek Revival to Italianate, the house includes characteristics of both with a colonnaded porch and bracketed cornice. The front door, outlined by stylish pilasters with inset paneled Doric columns and a bracketed entablature, has sidelights and a transom of etched ruby glass. The interior consists of a central hall, widening in the rear, with the typical two rooms on each side.

CARPENTER'S SHOP
401 DECATUR STREET

Located at the corner of North Decatur and Columbus Streets, a ca. 1915 storefront serves as a carpenter's shop for Old Alabama Town. One story with showcase windows, the masonry building was once a neighborhood café and later an appliance repair shop. Landmarks Foundation acquired it in the early 1980s and converted it for the present use. It is a work area and is not open to the public.

GLOSSARY

Antebellum—Period before the Civil War.

Chinking—A mixture of mud, chicken feathers, horse or mule hair, twigs, splinters—anything that might adhere and harden into a plaster placed between logs to fill cracks. (log cabin)

Cotton gin—A machine for separating cotton lint from seeds.

Cupola—A small dome or room with windows topping a roof. These were for decoration and, especially in the South, for ventilation as a trapdoor or a door in the cupola could be opened to allow hot air to rise. (Ware-Farley-Hood House)

Dogtrot house—A two-pen (room) structure with a roofed and floored open passageway between the pens. (Rose House and Yancey Dogtrot)

Federal—Style popular in the post–Revolutionary period, especially in the South. Slender columns on porticos, sometimes fanlights over the front doors, and delicate interior woodwork. (Martin-Barnes House)

Gingerbread—Wooden spool and fretwork used for decorative purposes from the development of the jigsaw in 1850s until the early twentieth century. (See cottages on the west side of the 300 block of North Hull Street.)

Greek Revival—If there is one style personifying the image of the South, it is Greek Revival. The style is characterized by boxed or round, fluted or smooth columns with variations of Doric, Ionic, or Corinthian capitals. Greek Revival columns are heavier and more massive than those of Federal style. (Thompson Mansion, Campbell Cottage, and Cook House)

Grist mill—A place for grinding grain into flour, meal, or grits; may be animal, water, or engine powered.

I-house—A two-story house that is one room deep (so that in profile it suggests the capital letter "I"). An early southern variation on the I-house often added low shed or lean-to rooms across the back (Rose House). Many times there was a balancing shed-roofed porch across the front as well. In a few instances the front was made very formal with classical features and even columns, though the tall, skinny basic "I" form is still evident from the sides as in the Molton House.

Italianate—A style derived from popular ideas of Italian architecture and prevalent in the South from 1850s to the 1880s. The style featured a low, hipped roof with wide overhanging bracketed eaves. The cornice was often detailed with decorative ventilator covers in Montgomery houses.(Cooper and Cram-Lakin cottages). Many Italianate houses had towers or rooftop cupolas (Ware-Farley-Hood House).

Lean-to—A one-story addition with a sloping roof, usually at rear of a house.

Log cabin—A house built of logs, either whole or split, with chinking in between.

Pole barn—A simple barn with open passage through the middle. The barn was constructed of poles with split logs or rough-hewn planks applied to form exterior walls.

Postbellum—Period following the Civil War.

Saddlebag—A two-room house with two front doors and a common chimney between the rooms. (Lakin, Molton, and Dorsey outbuildings and Cook House Cookhouse)

Shotgun house—A narrow house, one room in width, with rooms aligned one behind the other.

Tidewater cottage—A story-and-a-half cottage with chimneys at each gable end, often with dormer windows as well. The Tidewater-type cottage first occurred in colonial Virginia, and variations occur elsewhere in the Southeast. (Martin-Barnes House is an adaptation of the type. The Graves-Haigler House is a further variant that adds an inset porch beneath the front roof slope.)

Vernacular—Style of architecture peculiar to a particular culture or region; folk architecture.

THE LATCH STRING IS OUT

"The Latch String is Out," a saying that originated in the days when families secured their cabins by primitive means, was an open invitation to visit. The latch string manipulated a simple wooden or metal bar attached to the interior of the door; when the string was on the outside, anyone could lift the bar by pulling the string and pushing the door open. Everyone was welcome. When ready to retire for the night, the family pulled the string inside and made sure the bar was in its door-frame slot. Their home was then safe.

Old Alabama Town has the latch string out for you six days a week throughout the year. We will welcome you and see that you have a good time while learning about central Alabama's past. We hope you will encourage others to visit as well.

Old Alabama Town Information

Landmarks has a number of special events annually, including walking tours, lectures, seminars, exhibits, concerts, jam sessions, Christmas events, and children's activities.

The Reception Center, at 301 Columbus Street, is open from 8:30 to 4:30. Tickets are available from 9:00 to 3:00. Museum store hours are 8:30 to 4:30.

Group Tours

By prior arrangement, groups of ten or more may have a guide and receive a discount. There are special rates for our widely acclaimed school tours, which must be prescheduled. Call 334-240-4517 for arrangements.

Membership

Landmarks Foundation invites everyone to join. Benefits include free tours, guest passes, museum store discounts, free admission to some events, and reduced admission to others. Members also get that good feeling from helping to preserve Alabama's history and heritage.

For information about Old Alabama Town, please call 334-240-4500 or 888-240-1850.

SUGGESTIONS FOR FURTHER READING

Benton, Jeffrey C. *The Very Worst Road: Travellers' Accounts of Crossing Alabama's Old Creek Indian Territory, 1820–1847*. Eufaula: Historical Chattahoochee Commission of Alabama and Georgia, 1998.

Boyd, Minnie Clare. *Alabama in the Fifties: A Social Study*. New York: Columbia University, 1931.

Cash, W. J. *The Mind of the South*. New York: Alfred A. Knopf, 1941.

Duffee, Mary Gordon. *Sketches of Alabama*. Ed. Virginia Pounds Brown and Jane Porter Nabers. University: University of Alabama Press, 1970.

Flynt, Wayne. *Montgomery, An Illustrated History*. Woodland Hills, CA: Windsor Publications, 1980.

Gosse, Philip Henry. *Letters from Alabama*. Reprint, Birmingham: Overbrook House, 1983.

Griffith, Lucille. *Alabama: A Documentary History to 1900*. University: University of Alabama Press, 1972.

Jackson, Harvey H., III. *Rivers of History: Life on the Coosa, Tallapoosa, Cahaba, and Alabama*. Tuscaloosa: University of Alabama Press, 1995.

Jordon, Weymouth T. *Ante-bellum Alabama: Town and Country*. Reprint, University: University of Alabama Press, 1987.

Muskat, Beth Taylor, and Mary Ann Neeley. *The Way It Was, 1850–1930: Photographs of Montgomery and Her Central Alabama Neighbors*. Montgomery: Landmarks Foundation, 1985.

Neeley, Mary Ann. *Boll Weevil Review: Essays on Central Alabama*. Montgomery: Landmarks Foundation, 1995.

——— *Montgomery: Capital City Corners*. Charleston, SC: Arcadia Publishers, 1997.

Oliver, Thomas W. *A Narrative History of Cotton in Alabama and a Tour of the Old Alabama Town Gin*. Montgomery: Landmarks Foundation, 1992.

Owsley, Frank Lawrence. *Plain Folk of the Old South*. Baton Rouge: Louisiana State University Press, 1949.

Pickett, Albert James. *History of Alabama and Incidentally of Georgia and Mississippi*. Reprint, Baltimore: Clearfield, 2000.

Rabinowitz, Howard N. *Race Relations in the Urban South, 1865–1890*. Urbana: University of Illinois Press, 1980.

Rogers, William Warren, Jr. *Confederate Home Front: Montgomery During the Civil War*. Tuscaloosa: University of Alabama Press, 1999.

Rogers, William Warren. *The One-Gallused Rebellion: Agrarianism in Alabama 1865–1896*. Reprint, Tuscaloosa: University of Alabama Press, 2001.

Rogers, William Warren, Robert David Ward, Leah Rawls Atkins, and Wayne Flynt. *Alabama: The History of a Deep South State*. Tuscaloosa: University of Alabama Press, 1994.

Scott, John B., Jr. *Memories of the Mount: the Story of Mount Meigs, Alabama*. Montgomery: Black Belt Press, 1993.

Southerland, Henry DeLeon, Jr., and Jerry Elijah Brown. *The Federal Road through Georgia, the Creek Nation, and Alabama, 1806–1836*. Tuscaloosa: University of Alabama Press, 1989.

Woodward, Thomas S. *Woodward's Reminiscences of the Creek, or Muscogee Indians*. Reprint, Mobile: Southern University Press, 1965.